PROPHETIC
RESET

Books by Joshua Giles

Prophetic Forecast
Mantled for Greatness
Prophetic Reset

PROPHETIC
RESET

40 DAYS TO ALIGNING WITH GOD'S PLAN FOR YOUR LIFE

JOSHUA GILES

Chosen

a division of Baker Publishing Group
Minneapolis, Minnesota

© 2024 by Joshua Thomas Giles

Published by Chosen Books
Minneapolis, Minnesota
ChosenBooks.com

Chosen Books is a division of
Baker Publishing Group, Grand Rapids, Michigan

Printed in the United States of America

Library of Congress Cataloging-in-Publication Data
Names: Giles, Joshua, 1988- author.
Title: Prophetic reset : 40 days to aligning with god's plan for your life / Joshua Giles.
Description: Minneapolis : Chosen Books, a division of Baker Publishing Group, 2024. | Includes bibliographical references.
Identifiers: LCCN 2023048342 | ISBN 9780800772512 (cloth) | ISBN 9781493445639 (ebook)
Subjects: LCSH: Devotional exercises. | Christian life.
Classification: LCC BV4235.D4 G55 2024 | DDC 242/.2—dc23/eng/20240117
LC record available at https://lccn.loc.gov/2023048342

Cover Design: Rob Williams

The Author is represented by the literary agency of Embolden Media Group.

Baker Publishing Group publications use paper produced from sustainable forestry practices and postconsumer waste whenever possible.

24   25   26   27   28   29   30   7   6   5   4   3   2   1

CONTENTS

Week 3: Going Higher

Week 4: Restoration Is Here

Week 5: Reset for a Relaunch

Week 6: Redeeming the Time

Week 7: Strategic Spiritual Warfare

Week 8: Revolutionize Your Life

WEEK 1

Refresh

A Fresh Start

Bring us back to you! Give us a fresh start.
—Lamentations 5:21 CEV

The author of today's verse is believed to be Jeremiah, who had been crying out to the Lord for mercy because of the things he had seen happen to his nation, Israel. There was so much calamity. Their land had been stolen and left in ruins, children had been left fatherless, men had been shamed and hanged, wives were widowed, and daughters were raped. "Our hearts are sad; instead of dancing, we mourn. . . . We feel sick all over and can't even see straight" (Lamentations 5:15–17 CEV).

Carrying the grief of his people, the prophet cried out in bitter anguish to the Lord, saying, "How long will you allow the wicked to prevail and the righteous to suffer?" Maybe you've been in this same place where you've said, "Lord, how long will You allow those who operate wickedly to prosper? They are corrupt and deceitful. They have compromised and walked away from Your principles, and yet they prosper in all they do."

Maybe you've also seen people who faithfully do what the Lord asks and who live righteously deal with much warfare, one blow after another. "How long, O Lord, will You leave us in this place?" is the bitter anguish from your soul. As Jeremiah did, you, too, pray for mercy.

I believe that for you, God's grace and mercy are on the way. Despite the warfare, resistance, and demonic backlash you've been experiencing, you have stepped out to do what the Lord gave you the initiative to do. You have remained faithful. You have lived righteously. Don't ever believe God does not see you. But also, be aware. Be sober. The enemy hates the purpose of God in the life of the believer.

Whenever you step out in faith and obey the Lord, the hounds of hell will try to come after you to stop what God is doing in your life. But here's the good news: Those demonic spirits have no authority over you unless you allow them to. As the Scripture says, "No weapon formed against you shall prosper" (Isaiah 54:17).

So, as you cry out to God in the midst of your troubles, I hear Him say, *I am releasing to you a fresh start.* The Lord is bringing you back to Himself. He is calling you to a place of restoration and recovery and a place of safety so that you can start over. He knows that this season of your life has begun with difficulty.

I remember a particularly difficult season in my life that started off with much warfare. I received one attack after another. I dealt with it silently and with my prayer partners and those who are part of my team. We know, of course, that life has its challenges. Sometimes it rains, and sometimes the sun is shining. But this time, it seemed as if the enemy had stepped it up. As the days passed and we pressed into God more, I began to hear from others who were going through similar levels of warfare, attacks, and infirmity in their bodies. Whatever darkness Satan had released in the world the previous season, he had increased it in this one.

The Lord did not let me get too far into this battle and into intercession for others who were also battling before He stopped me to say, *Although this season has started off badly, I am going to turn the page and release a fresh start.*

Whenever we come to a place where we sense that God is leading us to a new season in our lives, we should take the time to assess what has happened since the last turning point. We should wait for a prophetic word or give language to what we hear the Lord saying. The phrase *fresh start* that God used to prophetically define this next moment means that God is going to hit the reset button, and this next leg of your journey will be as if you are starting a whole new season.

With this fresh start, you are entering another sphere of influence—another door. Opportunities are beginning to open for you right now. You will not be pigeonholed in the place that you have been. You will not remain stuck at the level you have been on.

As you start fresh with God, I decree that glory will return to Zion. Regardless of how things were going in the past, you will enter a period of celebration. You will dance during famine. You will rejoice in the midst of chaos. You will shout and give praise to God amid all the things you see going on around you. Decree this over this season and over your day today. Look for the small victories. Look for the small wins. Look for God's favor. Look for the ways in which He is restoring you, and declare that it is celebration time. You have entered a season of new harvest.

Renew your mind with this fresh perspective, and don't allow the enemy to steal your joy or your praise. Set your mind and spirit toward celebration. Will there still be attacks and chaos? Yes. Jesus said, "In this world you will have trouble. But take heart! I have overcome the world" (John 16:33 NIV). So no matter how grim things look around you, use your eyes of faith and rejoice in the midst of it. Decree, "God is giving me a fresh start."

Have faith and believe that, with God's help, you will continue to be effective in the assignment of the Lord on your life. You will see the hand of the Lord move. No matter how dark it gets, set your heart to rejoice anyway.

I decree that everything in your life is about to change for the better. I'm sharing with you what I've sensed from heaven in my time of prayer regarding what the Holy Spirit is doing right now. Everything in your life is about to change for the better as you yield to the will of God for your life. As you listen for the leading of the Holy Spirit, you will experience a fresh start.

This is the time to lean in and start again, to launch out again. I know you tried it before and it didn't work, but you will accomplish it this time. I know you built something, and it got knocked down. The enemy came after it, and you experienced loss. But the Lord says that you must build it again. Start fresh, and this time the momentum of God is going to be with you. You're going to see a spiritual momentum that will build in your favor.

PRAYER

Father, I come before You humbling myself under Your mighty hand, under Your Kingdom agenda, and under the assignment that You've placed on my life. Holy Spirit,

I want to be led by You. I want to be directed by You. I don't want to be led by my gifts, led by my flesh, or led by my selfish agenda. Father, I lay all those things down and make them part of the footstool of Jesus Christ. I lay all my desires at the cross. Teach me how to welcome the fresh start You are giving me. Show me how to begin again with Your hand of grace, mercy, and favor on my life. Let me do this not leaning on my own strength and understanding but depending on and surrendering to Yours. I pray this in Jesus' name, Amen.

"Bring Me Back to You!"

Bring us back to you! Give us a fresh start.

—Lamentations 5:21 CEV

As God brings you to a fresh start and begins to set things right for you, the first half of our Day 1 verse says you must get back in alignment with Him. "Bring me back to You" must be the cry of your heart. The time of the show, the program, and the performance is over. Your desire must be purely for the presence of God, the weight of His glory, the beauty of His face, and the power of His Spirit to become all the more evident in your life. The fresh start I introduced on Day 1 is about coming back to the Bible and falling in love with the Word of God again. It's about coming back to the altar and laying yourself and all your cares at the feet of Jesus. It's about coming back to prayer.

With all your serving and doing, with all your pouring out of gifts, with all your intercession and ministry, you may have found yourself depleted. You may have even been drifting away from the purity of God's plans and purposes for your life. This is no judgment. It happens to the best of us. This is why God calls us back to Himself—to be refreshed by the simple but powerful things that renew us and reestablish our faith.

Oftentimes we ask God about the next, new thing He wants to do. We want Him to tell us something we've never heard before or to give us something He's never given before. But sometimes before we can move ahead into the new thing, the Lord must bring us back to the basics, back to Him—the beauty, the holiness, and the simple magnitude of His presence.

We must come back to our first love. Revelation 2:4–5 says, "You have left your first love. Remember therefore from where you have fallen; repent and do the first works." The word *repent* here means "to change one's mind," "to think differently," or "to reconsider."[1]

Repentance is also about our making a clear decision to go in a different direction than we had been going previously. In other words, you were going one way—and perhaps it was a way that God had shown you to go in the last season—but as He takes you higher in Him, there is a new place He wants to take you that requires a new set of directions. We can miss this change of direction. We must repent, or be willing to change our minds, to think differently than we had about something. We must stop going in the direction we had been going so that we can be rerouted on the new path God has designated for this stage of our journey.

Repentance is about recognizing our sin, which is simply missing the mark. Sometimes we think of sin in terms of what the darkest and most deviant actions in our Christian values or culture are. Sin does include those things, but it is also the simplest action of getting out of step with God. Often, these are things only you and God would know. You aren't breaking any laws, neither are you necessarily sinning against anyone else. But in the most intimate, private things, God whispers to your spirit, *Have you been truly faithful to hear and do all I command?* Only you and God know this. The reason He calls us back is so that we can say, "Search me, O God, and know my heart" (Psalm 139:23). When we are open and humble enough to confess the things that God reveals, His mercy, grace, forgiveness, and love are right there to get us back in right standing with Him.

And so, looking back at today's verse, what are the first works?

Think back to the time when you first came into relationship with God. What did you spend most of your time doing in His presence? For many believers, this is a time full of excitement about getting to know all they can about God by reading His Word. It's praying about everything. It's asking God to reveal Himself, to help them understand His ways, to live in a way that is pleasing to Him. The first moments with God are full of reverence, worship, and awe. Our desire for the Lord is unquenchable—a time much like the psalmist David wrote: "One thing I have desired of the LORD, that will I seek: that I may dwell in the house of the LORD all the days of my life, to behold the beauty of the LORD, and to inquire in His temple" (Psalm 27:4).

Do you remember?

The Lord is calling us back to a time with Him just like when we first believed. This will be a time when the Lord says, *I'm bringing you back in order to shoot you forward.* There are moments when we are in alignment with the Holy Spirit—times when He's about to shoot us forward. But in order for us to go forward, we often have to go back first.

This is what the author sang in Lamentations. He said, "Bring us back to you." Somewhere between living out God's call on our lives, caring for loved ones, being on time for work, and maintaining friendships, businesses, and ministries—doing all the doing—we can drift away. We drift away from prayer. We drift away in our heart from God and others. We drift away when it comes to our relationship with the Father. There is nothing more important than our relationship with the Holy Spirit, and there is nothing more important than our relationship with Jesus Christ. So, yes, you need this fresh start, this clean slate.

PRAYER

Father, I pray that You would usher me, by Your Spirit, back to You, my first love. Bring me back to the way I was when I first received You. Let my heart burn again with a passion to know You and Your ways, to think differently about what You require from me as You supernaturally reset my life. I repent and turn away from the pleasures of life that put You left of center in my heart. Thank You for calling me back to You. In Jesus' name, Amen.

Get Ready;
It's Going to Rain

Go up, eat and drink; for there is the sound of abundance of rain.

—1 Kings 18:41

In 1 Kings 18, we find the prophet Elijah making a declaration that it is going to rain *in the middle of a drought* that he had prophesied three years before. He had just won a showdown at Mount Carmel against the prophets of Baal to prove that the God of Israel is the One True God. The people watched as fire from heaven came and licked up the twelve pots of precious water Elijah told them to pour on the altar. I imagine this water was from the reserve they had been storing to keep themselves marginally clean and hydrated during this terrible drought. They stood there and watched it go up in flames. A victory, yes, but what were they going to drink, bathe in, and water their fields and livestock with? Now Elijah comes with another word from the Lord: It is going to rain.

The problem with this word is that there is not a cloud in sight—it is as dry as ever. It seems that the Lord always has us start something when it looks as though nothing is going on around us, when it looks as though nothing is going to happen for us. The Lord gives the mandate to declare rain when it's dry.

He gives you the vision to start something when you don't have the money or resources. He gives you a glimpse of delivering people when you aren't seeing breakthrough and are oppressed. He tells you of your prosperous and victorious future when you are in lack and in poverty. This is what God does: He finds you in your lowest moment and gives you the word for your next.

And so, in the middle of the drought, God sends the word through the prophet Elijah that it's going to rain—even though there was not a cloud in sight. Elijah sends his servant to go look. "'Go up now, look toward the sea.' So he went up and looked, and said, 'There is nothing'" (verse 43).

If this happened now, people would be calling Elijah a false prophet. They would question his anointing. "How could he be prophesying rain when there's not a cloud in sight and it's still dry?"

Imagine if you were that servant and this great seasoned prophet is telling you, "The Lord says it's going to rain. Go and look for the cloud." You go, look, and come back to him saying, "I still don't see it." The servant did this over and over; Elijah kept prophesying.

There's a lesson in this: If you have a word from the Lord, never stop prophesying and decreeing what He has said. People will mock you. They may resist you. There will be demonic strongholds and enemies that come against you. The very reason they are coming against you is because the devil is afraid of the word of the Lord in your mouth. Those demonic spirits are afraid of your ability to declare what God has said. I'm sure that you know this is true from personal experience. You likely have been beaten in the spirit, taking hit after hit because you kept prophesying. I encourage you today to keep prophesying and never stop.

Elijah kept speaking it, and he kept sending the servant back. The fourth time the servant came back, he said, "I still don't see anything. There is not even a cloud in the sky."

You or I would have given up at this point. We may have said, "Well, okay, this prophet has missed it. He was accurate before, but he's not accurate now. The Lord used him at one time, but he is off on this one. We are still in a drought."

We must remember that the Lord always gives the word before we see it manifest in the natural. As you enter this fresh start with God, you will need to be able to walk by faith and not by sight. God will say some things to you that are not going to make sense. The Holy Spirit is going to speak a word in your spirit, and it may not make sense. It's not going to fit your budget or your schedule. But when you hear the voice of the Lord, you have to move. You will not have time to second guess. You will not have time to think, "Well, Lord, is this really You?" You will not have time to go on a fifty-day fast. When you hear the voice of the Lord speaking to you, you must move by faith and not by sight. If you pay too much attention to what's going on around you, you will miss the open door in this season.

Imagine if the servant stopped and said, "Well, no, Elijah. You missed it this time. There is no rain coming. I don't see a cloud. You keep sending me to look for something that's invisible. You keep sending me to look in the sky and nothing is there." But he didn't. He remained invested in sticking with the process even though he may not have understood what was happening.

Elijah sends the servant a fifth time and a sixth time. From the first time Elijah sent the servant to check the skies, the Bible says that Elijah was on the ground with his head between his knees (see verse 42), meaning that Elijah was in deep intercession. He was in a position and place of prayer. He was groaning in his spirit. He was laboring in intercession to see the manifestation of what the Lord had said.

There is a place you can come into with the Father where you partner with the Holy Spirit. You begin to partner with Him to see His agenda manifest in the earth. That's exactly what Elijah was doing when he was in that place of prayer and intercession. He was down on his knees. He was partnering with the Holy Spirit to see the manifestation of what God had said.

You may be at a place where you feel as if you want to give up. Do not let go. Don't give up because you are almost there. If you make the decision to come into partnership with the Holy Spirit, you are going to see heaven open for you.

The Bible says that Elijah sent the servant six times to look in the sky, and each time the servant saw nothing. After the seven time, the servant finally came back and said, "There is a cloud, as small as a man's hand, rising out of the sea!" (verse 44).

This cloud was small. How would rain even come from a cloud so small? The Lord told me that part of this fresh start will release you from what has been holding you back. You will not be stuck in the drought. He knows your story. You put your hand to the plow in one season, and it wasn't productive for you. You started something in one season, and it didn't amount to anything. You tried to build it, you tried to start it, you tried to move ahead in it, and it didn't work out for you. But the Lord said that as He gives you a new start, you will experience an anointing to build it again. You will put your hand back to the plow, and you will build it again.

The Lord gave you a vision. Maybe it didn't work before, but it is going to work this time. Maybe you stepped out in it, and nothing came together for you. But when you do it this time, it will come to pass.

PRAYER

Father, I thank You for this word over my life. I hear You saying, "Don't quit." I prophesy over my own life that rain is coming. Even in the midst of famine, I will prosper. I will see the hand of the Lord move as I receive this fresh start. I decree it, I speak it, and I prophesy it. In Jesus' name, Amen.

Everything Great Starts Small

Do not despise these small beginnings, for the LORD rejoices to see the work begin.

—Zechariah 4:10 NLT

As I sought the Lord in prayer concerning how we should approach this fresh start, He told me, *Do not overlook the small thing. Don't overlook the small thing because out of a small thing comes greatness. Out of the small seed comes a big oak tree.* Maybe part of the challenge with how we started this season came because we were looking for something huge. What the Lord is doing is going to start in the form of a seed. It's going to start small.

Get ready for the small thing, because within the small thing is greatness. The Bible says that we should not despise the day of small beginnings. Just because it's small doesn't mean it's not great. Just because the vision looks small or the ministry you have looks small does not mean that greatness is not coming from it.

I'm prophesying to you that with this new start, the big thing you are about to experience is coming in the small thing. The Lord says that the next big thing that's coming in your life is going to show up small like a seed, so don't despise the small thing.

The next part of this caution is that the Lord rejoices when we start something. The Lord literally rejoices at the start. I want you to get this because we've been discussing a fresh start. Do you understand that when you start on anything that the Lord has put in your spirit—a vision He's put in your spirit, an idea He's given you, a God-given assignment, a project for the Lord that you are carrying out—the moment you start it, the Bible says that the Lord rejoices at its beginning. He rejoices at the start of it. This means that as you are embarking on a fresh start, as you're building it again, as you are relaunching your assignment, as you're stepping out on faith in that ministry, or as you're stepping out on faith in that business, heaven is throwing a party for you. Heaven rejoices when the work begins.

See, the enemy tries to discourage us not to start. He tries to make us think we are not qualified, that we don't have it all together—and none of us has it together without God's help. Still, the enemy works to amplify our weaknesses and past failures to make us think we're not equipped for the task or assignment. "You're not really anointed for that," he may taunt. "Why are you doing that thing? People are going to laugh at you."

What I have found is that the enemy always fights the start of an assignment because he knows that if you can push past the obstacles and get it started, you will experience momentum. So, he fights you the hardest at the beginning so that you won't pick up the momentum. That momentum will silence him and leave his weapons against you powerless. He fights against you the worst when you step out in faith to do what the Lord has told you to do. He's warring against you because he knows that if you start, the Lord will rejoice.

The moment you say, "Lord, I will do the thing You asked me to do," He begins to rejoice. Why? Because you just broke through a barrier. As the Lord rejoices and heaven throws a party, so will you. You are coming into a time of celebration. You've seen some tough times, and there has been so much spiritual activity. But you are about to rise up and push back. You will embrace this fresh start, and you will not stop.

I come into agreement with you and command a ceasefire, a period of reprieve in the name of Jesus. We will not be intimidated when we see backlash, when we see the enemy try to come against us to make things worse. Together, we declare that the storm is over, and we are being given a fresh start. Even in the face of chaos, we will celebrate the start of a new thing. In the face of calamity, we will see God's grace and mercy. Together, let us declare that our mourning has turned into celebrating, right now, in Jesus' name. We will not overlook the small things God brings to us. We will look at every new opportunity and every new door through the eyes of faith, and we will know that what begins small can be multiplied into something great.

PRAYER

Lord, I thank You for the small things You bring into my life. I pray that as I follow You into this season of reset my eyes will be open to see Your greatness, Your favor, and Your promotion in the little things. I also pray that You will strengthen my heart as I set out to begin again. Let me not shrink back at the enemy's empty threats. Thank You for celebrating the things I start. May I remain in alignment, never taking my eyes off You. In Jesus' name, Amen.

A New Season of Harvest

I will restore to you the years that the swarming locust has eaten,
the crawling locust, the consuming locust, and the chewing
locust.

—Joel 2:25

When the word of the Lord in Joel 2 came to the people
of Israel, they were in the middle of one of the greatest droughts and famines that had come upon them. On top
of that, a plague of locust had eaten their entire harvest. It was
dire. Not only were they experiencing an economic downturn,
but they were also experiencing a drought and a famine. In the
midst of this dark time, the prophecy in verses 25–29 came:

"So I will restore to you the years that the swarming locust has
eaten, the crawling locust, the consuming locust, and the chewing locust, My great army which I sent among you. You shall
eat in plenty and be satisfied, and praise the name of the LORD
your God, who has dealt wondrously with you; and My people
shall never be put to shame. Then you shall know that I am in

the midst of Israel: I am the LORD your God and there is no other. My people shall never be put to shame. And it shall come to pass afterward that I will pour out My Spirit on all flesh; your sons and your daughters shall prophesy, your old men shall dream dreams, your young men shall see visions. And also on My menservants and on My maidservants I will pour out My Spirit in those days."

The fulfillment of this word was recorded in Acts 2 when on the harvest holiday, called Pentecost or the Feast of Weeks, the Holy Spirit poured Himself out on those followers of Jesus who had been awaiting His arrival in the Upper Room after Jesus had ascended back to heaven.[2] Pentecost being known as the Feast of Weeks is significant in Scripture because the Feast of Weeks is a celebration of a grain harvest. It is an agricultural Thanksgiving-type holiday. It falls fifty days after Passover.

I want you to catch that the Lord would choose to pour His Spirit out on an agricultural harvest holiday. Why is that? Because it signifies an entrance into a season of harvest. A fresh start prepares you for a coming harvest of those things that God has promised in your life. Pentecost is the announcement of a fresh start. It is the announcement that a page is turning in the spirit realm.

But for many believers, Pentecost is a commemoration of the Acts 2 outpouring, and we celebrate it in our churches once a year. In our present-day celebrations, we see some of the exponential growth and miracles that the New Testament Church experienced. I believe the Lord moves in those services, and it isn't so that we can say that we had an amazing experience. We dance, we shout, and we praise God. We are undone by what He did. But that level of praise and demonstration of the power of God is not to be contained to one Sunday or to one experience. Pentecost should be seen as an announcement from heaven that we have stepped over into an *era* of Pentecost—not just a day once a year.

Pentecost was never supposed to stop. The Lord urged me to tell you this: You have stepped over into a season of Pentecost, a season of the new harvest. It will not just be a one-day or one-time experience. You are coming into a fresh start, or what I'm naming a place that is called fresh. It's new. It's never been seen before. It's never happened before. You've never been in this place before. It is your own Pentecost where God pours His Spirit over and in you, bringing you to a fresh start.

With this outpouring comes restoration. The Lord says, "I will restore to you the years that the swarming locust has eaten." To *restore* something means "to bring back to or put back into a former or original state." It means to "renew," to "revive" or "revitalize," to "return to an original state after depletion or loss."[3] This is what I believe the Lord is doing for you as He resets your life, gives you a fresh start, and brings you back to Himself.

Like the people of Israel, you cannot look at what is going on around you. You must take the word that the Lord is speaking to you. You may be in one of the worst situations in your life, but I'm prophesying that, in the midst of it, you will see the hand of the Lord move. You will be restored.

I took this passage of Scripture to the Lord in prayer, and He showed me this strange vision of a swarm of insects. I was not aware of what kind of insect it was, but I saw it as a swarm. The Lord said, *In the natural, you're going to see this swarm hit news outlets. These swarms are going to gather in different areas. They will be so massive that they will get the attention of*

31

the media and those who are around. Even in certain industries such as agriculture, you're going to hear of it. When you see this swarm form, tell the people that it will be a sign that, even though the plagues will come, I will restore the years.

The Lord wants you to know that despite the swarm that comes, despite the attack of the enemy, you will prevail. Even though the weapon will be formed, you will prevail. What you may have lost in the last season is being restored as you enter a time of recovery, renewal, and restoration. This will be a time when the Lord says, *I will restore your years.*

PRAYER

Father, I thank You for this word of restoration. I receive Your refreshing and receive the season of Pentecost to which You are bringing me. Pour Your Spirit out over me, and never let the fire of Your Spirit die out. I don't want Pentecost just for one day; I want to experience the harvest of this new season for as long as You would allow it. Thank You for restoring the years that I've lost. Help me to be a good steward over the increase You are bringing to my life. In Jesus' name, Amen.

WEEK 2

A Holy Convocation

Consecration:
Sound the Trumpets

Speak to the children of Israel, saying: "In the seventh month, on the first day of the month, you shall have a sabbath-rest, a memorial of blowing of trumpets, a holy convocation. You shall do no customary work on it; and you shall offer an offering made by fire to the LORD."

—Leviticus 23:24–25

In today's verse, we find God speaking to the people of Israel about what is known as the Feast of Trumpets, which is one of the high holy times on God's calendar. During this time, the Lord would instruct the trumpets to be sounded. In those days there were at least two types of trumpets that could be sounded, depending on the occasion.

The first one was the shofar, which you may know is the ram's horn. It had to go through a specific process to be blown. This trumpet, or shofar, would release a sound over the people to celebrate and to commemorate. At other times, it would be blown to let the people know there was war. Then there were other times the trumpet sounded to let the people know that there was a gathering or a solemn assembly that God was calling together.

I believe the Body of Christ will experience the sounding of the trumpet that signal all these things at one time—war, God calling us to a solemn assembly, and celebration as we collect the spoils from the war in which He's led us to victory. We'll explore more about what God is saying to us in this reset about each of these concepts as we continue through this week's devotions.

The second type of trumpets that would sound in ancient Israel were the silver trumpets, which was symbolic of redemption. Whenever you see a silver trumpet mentioned in Scripture, understand that it represents redemption—God bringing His people back to the place they were before a loss. The sounding of the silver trumpet is an announcement of salvation. Its sounding could also be a sign of judgment—the Lord's judgment of matters and situations.[1] And there are situations that are in the balance right now upon which God is deliberating.

So as the Lord led the people of Israel out of Egypt, He inaugurated the Feast of Trumpets, and it was very important for several reasons:

1. It was a time of *consecration*. The Lord would send a call out to His people to gather and consecrate themselves for the new thing into which they were about to walk.

2. It was a time of *crossover*. It was a period where the calendar and the literal time was shifting. We see this in Exodus 12:1–2. I'll come back to this verse in a moment.

3. It was a time of *celebration* and remembrance of all the things God had done up until that point.

Could the time we will spend together over these forty days be one of these times for you personally? Could this be a time when the Lord is calling you back to Himself to consecrate you and for you to repent as you prepare to shift to the next phase of your journey with Him? I believe it is.

Notice I used the word *shift*. Keep that word in your spirit as we read Exodus 12:1–2:

> Now the Lord spoke to Moses and Aaron in the land of Egypt, saying, "This month shall be your beginning of months; it shall be the first month of the year to you."

When the Lord brought His people out of Egyptian bondage, the first thing that He did was to change their calendar and shift their time. Life had been lived according to a solar calendar, which is similar to the calendar we use throughout the world right now. The Lord was resetting their time based on the new start He was giving them. Essentially, He was saying, *Even though the rest of the world is in this particular month, I'm going to cause this to be the first month for you. I'm changing the entire calendar, and you will now operate off a lunar calendar.* God started a new year for His people—a year that started in concert with their liberation from bondage. This new year signified a new place and position for His people.

God is sounding the trumpet and calling you to Himself, and in this time, He is going to reset you so that you are realigned with His plan for your life. What is it that you know He's been telling you to start? What has He been asking you to invest time or energy into that you've avoided or put off? You may not need to hear something new from God—though He can release a powerful new word to you.

This may not be a time for you to go into deep moments of worship, to shout, or to become overwhelmed in His presence. This may be a time for you to be still and listen for what God is saying, to be realigned with things He's revealed to you before, and to be reactivated to do the things He's commanded.

Consecration is a time for you to resubmit yourself to God—your time, your plans, your agendas, everything. It is a time to recommit yourself to God and the plans He has for your life. Consecration is all about you being devoted to doing what God wants. During this time, as our verse from today says, you shall do no customary work. In other words, you will set your plans and agendas aside. This is your "Yes, God," and "Speak, Lord," moment. As you surrender to Him, He can then begin to reorganize or shift your time and priorities so that you are able to focus on and do what is pleasing to Him.

Yes, God wants to shift you, but you must surrender. Surrender and obedience come first—before consecration, crossing over, or celebration. The people of Israel first had to surrender to God's plan to set them free from the oppression of Egypt. They then had to do what He said in order to be brought out. This process of submission and obedience was not as easy as many of us might think it should have been. Who wouldn't want to be set free from slavery? But the Bible says that the people were afraid of how life would be if they left Egypt. They had become comfortable in their bondage; however, their desire for freedom grew stronger than the fear of the unknown. God sent a deliverer. They obeyed and followed Moses as he followed God, and they were led out. Once they were free, God then shifted their time and gave them a fresh start.

God is calling you out, too. You have been delivered and set free. The trumpet is sounding. Your appointment to meet with God is here. Will you begin to surrender to God today so that He can change your calendar?

PRAYER

Father, I thank You for Your word to me today. I thank You for desiring to spend time with me, to pour into me, and to help me start fresh with You. I see that You are shifting me, and I surrender to Your plans. I reconsecrate myself to You this day. Lord, let Your will be done in my life. I don't want to hear from man. I don't desire to hear from the flesh, nor do I desire to commit any longer to human agendas. I submit my plans to You.

Holy Spirit, I want to hear from You. Speak, Lord. As Your word comes to me, I will listen and obey. I want to cross over into this new season with You and Your agenda leading me. Thank You for all You've done in my life. I look forward to this new season. In Jesus' name, Amen.

Crossing Over: Healing from the Past

He also brought them out with silver and gold, and there was none feeble among His tribes.

—Psalm 105:37

The next thing that the Lord did when He brought His people out of Egyptian bondage was to heal their bodies. When you look in rabbinical literature and commentaries regarding the things God did upon Israel's exodus from Egypt, you'll find that one of the greatest miracles was not the parting of the Red Sea. Yes, their backs were up against the wall and there was no way out. Yes, it was miraculous how the Lord parted the seas for them. But it was not the greatest miracle.

Being in slavery for as long as they had been, being beaten, malnourished, and overworked, many of them were not in the best health or in the best condition. Some suffered from various illnesses and broken bones. And so, one of the greatest miracles

God performed for them as they were leaving was to instantly heal their bodies.

Whenever the Lord causes us to exit one year or one period of time and enter into a new year or a new period of time, I believe that there is divine healing that has been set up for us. It is very possible for you to come out of a place or out of a situation that was devastating for you and have that trauma still be with you.

God may shift your time and do all kinds of supernatural things to bring you to a new place and time but without His healing power working in your life, you can still be stuck in a place of hurt or trauma. The Lord has to then shift your timing and bring you spiritually out of the place you've been in. This is what He did for Israel. As He did this, He also healed them instantly from the trauma of Egypt.

Maybe you are coming to these forty days holding up your health to the Lord and petitioning Him for healing. You may be sick in body or broken in your spirit, but I believe that as you seek the Lord, reconsecrating yourself before Him during this appointed time, a wave and an anointing for healing will be released to you.

Is it wisdom you need to sustain good health? Do you need better understanding of what foods you should eat and what activities will bring vitality to your body so that you can carry out God's will more effectively? Do you need a reversal in the doctor's diagnosis? Do you need instant healing?

Has this season begun with unusual hardship spiritually or emotionally? You've been crying out to the Lord, praying, "God, how is this going to happen? When is it going to happen?" It may be that the situations and trials you've faced have been tougher than you faced at any other time in your life, and it is breakthrough or inner healing that you need. Whatever healing you need during this season, I'm decreeing that as you cross over, healing will manifest and break out in your life.

I hear the Lord saying, *I am the God who heals you, and I am healing you right now*. I can sense it so strongly, that as you've come aside with God during these forty days, you will get a new start, a reset for your health—body, mind, and spirit. God loves you and wants you to prosper and be in health. He knows the desires of your heart. He knows the things you are passionate about, and He knows you need to be well in all areas to accomplish all that He has set before you.

If you hold on to the word of the Lord, you will come out on the other side with a testimony that God raised you up from that bed of sickness, from the inner pain that only you know about. Receive this word. You will see the demonstrated power of God, the glory of God in your life. You will testify!

PRAYER

Father, I pray and release divine breakthroughs of healing over me. I pray that You will cause waves of healing to come physically, emotionally, and on a soul level for every area of my life. Heal me from battle wounds and oppression. Make me new. As You heal me from the inside out, I come into this time of consecration and repentance willingly. Demonstrate Your power in my life and let my crossing over from my spiritual Egypt to my land of promise be a testament to Your glory. Thank You for leading, guiding, protecting, and restoring me. In Jesus' name, Amen.

Crossing Over:
The End of a Thing

Better is the end of a thing than the beginning thereof: and the
patient in spirit is better than the proud in spirit.

—Ecclesiastes 7:8 KJV

For the next several days and months, I believe God is going
to help shift things in your life. These forty days will be a
time of new beginnings for you. In this time, you may see many
closures happening in the spirit realm. You may experience relationships coming to an end and other things that marked the
last season expiring. You may wonder if something has gone
wrong, if you did something wrong, or if the enemy has found
an open door. I encourage you: Do not see it as an attack. It
will not be that. Instead, it will be the Lord's doing.

As you cross over into this new place that God is bringing
you, there will be an end to things you've been toiling with and
working on. The Lord says, *I'm going to close that and open
something new*. Many times, we are afraid of something ending.

We are afraid to walk away from a particular thing or situation. There's an even greater fear when a relationship comes to an end. Keep in mind that I am not telling you to walk away from everything in your life. I'm telling you to walk away from everything except that which the Lord ordains. Wait for Him to lead you in the areas where the time of your involvement is coming to an end. When the Lord brings closure to a situation in your life, trust that He is also bringing about your next new thing. If He closes a job, trust that as you leave that job, you'll be walking into another one soon.

Oftentimes, our fear of the closing of a thing comes because we don't know what's next. In these times, it is important that we raise the level of our faith to believe that God has what is next for us. Our faith increases when we mark with thanksgiving the times God has brought us through in the past. Faith increases when we immerse ourselves in the biblical testimony of those God healed, delivered, and set free, those He brought out of darkness into His marvelous light, and those He liberated from the hand of the enemy.

If He did it once, He'll do it again. You must hold on to this truth in times like these more than ever. It is in these times that things seem to get worse before they get better. There are feelings and emotions at play as we end assignments or relationships at God's direction. Through it all, we must know that He is walking with us. God has already mapped out our future. He says in Jeremiah, "I knew you before I formed you in your mother's womb. Before you were born I set you apart and appointed you as my prophet to the nations" (Jeremiah 1:5 NLT).

Your new season—your prophetic reset—has already been determined. God determined it before you were born. He determined your steps and ordered them before you came into this earth (see Psalm 37:23). Trust and believe God that this next season has already been mapped out, that it has already been laid out before you. God has good things prepared for you. Ask Him to let you in on His plans so that you can see in the spirit the good things that have been prepared for you. I can see it happening for you even now, and I want you to catch this word.

God says, *I have good things prepared for My people.* There are things you've never thought of that will happen in the coming days and weeks. The Bible says, "Eye has not seen, nor ear heard, nor have entered into the heart of man the things which God has prepared for those who love Him" (1 Corinthians 2:9). There are things that will happen to you as you cross over into the next place God is calling you that your eyes have never seen and your ears have never heard. You will have cause to rejoice.

So don't be afraid, and don't get stuck in the places or relationships from which God is moving you on. Embrace His direction as He leads you from one level to the next. Your time in His presence to know just what He is doing will be crucial. He may have a Moses, Joshua, or Caleb come into your life to help you cross over from the old into the new.

Higher levels of worship, prayer, Bible study, and maybe even fasting may become your regular practice during this time so that you don't miss this move of God in your life. Approach this time of consecration as a time of listening for the voice of God and as a time to build your faith to step out into the new thing God is preparing for you.

Get ready for a time of rejoicing. This is a time when your divine endings will lead you to greater things. Truly the end of a thing will be greater than its beginning, and you can rejoice as you cross over from old into new because you will know that God has ordered your steps.

PRAYER

God, I thank You for directing me through the necessary endings and closure I need to move forward. I thank You for directing me into new and greater things. I pray that Your Spirit will be with me more than ever before. Cover me on every side. Speak so that I may hear Your instructions. Empower me with the grace to do as You command. I look forward with great expectation to walking into a season of rejoicing as I look back at all You've brought me to and through. In Jesus' name, Amen.

Crossing Over: Favor and Supernatural Transfer

And the LORD had given the people favor in the sight of the Egyptians, so that they granted them what they requested. Thus they plundered the Egyptians.

—Exodus 12:36

As God brought His people out of Egypt, He not only healed them and shifted their time, but He also caused the Egyptians to look favorably upon them. The New Living Translation states, "They gave the Israelites whatever they asked for," so much so that "they stripped the Egyptians of their wealth!"

When they were exiting one place, exiting the bondage they had been in, and exiting the time they had been used to keeping and were stepping into a new spiritual year or season, the Lord allowed them to get everything they opened their mouths and asked for. They asked the Egyptians for substance, for gold and silver. The Bible says that they stripped the Egyptians of their wealth, meaning that a supernatural transfer happened.

Let me tell you that there are some things that the past season still owes you. You are not going to cross over into this next season without the past season paying you back for what it owes you. Get ready to see the "Egyptians"—whoever or whatever they represent in your life—stripped of their wealth. Get ready to see the enemies you have fought, those who withstood you, be stripped of their wealth. They will have to give you what they owe.

I'm believing this reset for you will be all about payback— also known as recompense or restitution. This is not something for you to go after in your own wisdom, strategy, or strength, because the Lord says, "It is mine to avenge; I will repay" (Deuteronomy 32:35 NIV; cf. Romans 12:19). God's justice, His way of making things right, is far better than yours. Let Him do it. Let Him turn things for your good.

As the Lord shifts you into a new time and season, you will be set up to receive pay, or compensation, for everything you suffered. This is a prophetic word. God is going to pay you for every, single thing you endured in secret. You may have had to suffer and couldn't tell anybody. You've gone through situations you couldn't voice. You couldn't go to people in public. You didn't have anyone to turn to. But the Lord says, *In the midst of that suffering, I will reward you*. There is a reward of the glory of the Lord that's about to come upon your life because of the tribulation or trial that you've come through.

The Camels Are Coming!

God is about to pay you back for the things you've had to endure. He is going to give you restitution, meaning that whatever is owed to you will be paid back. God is going to make you whole in whatever way you've been broken, and whatever was stolen will be returned. The Bible says, "When [a thief] is found, he must restore sevenfold; he may have to give up all the substance of his house" (Proverbs 6:31). We know who the thief is. We know his whole mission is to steal, kill, and destroy (see John 10:10), but God says, *Get ready to get it back.*

In addition to restitution, I want you to hear me by the Spirit that you are entering into a time when God is going to transfer to you the wealth that has been stored up by the wicked. You may have heard me talk about this during my live social media broadcasts, but in case you haven't, I wanted to include the revelation for you here. "The multitude of camels shall cover your land, the dromedaries of Midian and Ephah; all those from Sheba shall come; they shall bring gold and incense, and they shall proclaim the praises of the LORD" (Isaiah 60:6).

In the Spirit, I see that the camels are coming, and they are loaded with resources for you. Camels represent abundance. They represent the wealth of the wicked that was laid up now being given to you—the just, the righteous. The coming of the camels represents a transfer where the Lord takes something off of one individual and places it on a different individual. I declare that this is what is happening right now for you in this season of crossover and of your fresh start.

If you invest in the stock market or other investment options and you align yourself in obedience to the will of the Father, you will see a transfer of wealth take place. You may have seen history-making moments in the stock market in the past, but the Lord says that you will see another record broken. What will look like a new low will be a sign to those of us that are in the Body of Christ that money is shifting hands. It's going to be a sign, as in the days of ancient Israel, of the Egyptians being stripped of their wealth.

There are those who have been wealthy, but God says, *There are new millionaires rising up*. I don't prophesy this or say these kinds of things often, because this transfer is all about God's glory and the expansion of His Kingdom. For the people wanting to build empires and monuments in their own name, this isn't for them. But for you, the one who wants to see the name of the Lord magnified, get ready to see new Kingdom believers made into millionaires and multimillionaires to advance the Kingdom of God.

Material wealth is not the only way God can move His Kingdom forward. There will also be transfers of anointing and influence. You may be one to whom God transfers the anointing, influence, or notoriety that someone else was occupying. Their period of holding a certain position may be over, and the Lord is now raising you up to fill that space.

This season of transfer is massive and may not look like what you expect, so be open to whatever God may be transferring. His ways are not our ways, and His thoughts are not our thoughts; therefore, we must align with His vision concerning our purposes and callings and what must be transferred to us to accomplish them.

As you are proven faithful, yielded, and submitted to the Father, the time of transfer is upon you. There will be enemies that will try to stand in your way, but hear me by the Spirit, there is nothing that they will be able to do because of the massive transfer that is coming.

Your season of restitution is here!

PRAYER

Father, I thank You for your deliverance from the past and the trauma that came with the things I've endured. Thank You for holding me up with Your mighty right hand through it all. As I cross over into this new era with You, I thank You in advance for the transfer of resources that are coming to me so that I may accomplish Your plans and help expand Your Kingdom influence. I receive Your restitution and welcome the new place into which You are bringing me. In Jesus' name, Amen.

Celebration: It's Revival Time

After two days He will revive us; on the third day He will raise us up, that we may live in His sight.

—Hosea 6:2

As we've discovered this week, this forty-day reset will be a season of divine recovery for you—your season of restitution and restoration. When God speaks about restoration and recovery, He means that the pieces of your soul that have been broken are about to come back together. It means that God is going to breathe new life back into you. When the Lord restores you, He breathes life into your being. He revives your soul. In other words, you are heading into a season of revival—one you have never experienced before.

As you seek God daily in His Word, in worship, and in prayer, and as you set your mind on Him and the things that please Him, you are going to see a revival of your vision, dreams, and assignments. Go back to those secret dreams and desires you know God laid on your heart and lift them up to Him again. Get your prayer journal and take notes on what He's saying to you. Have faith and trust Him, because what may have looked dead is about to receive new life. You may have thought your church or ministry was dead. It's not dead. It's about to receive new life. You are going to see it happen over the next several months.

As you delight yourself in Him, you will find that this holy convocation God has called you to will be a season of revival for you and everything that concerns you. You will see it happen in your church and community, your workplace, and your home. You are in for a mass revival.

If you have felt yourself drifting away from God in recent months, you are going to come back to Him over the course of this season. The Lord is calling you back to Himself. Perhaps you have been in a period where you feel as though the anointing God placed on you has diminished or is no longer there. It's about to come on you again, but this time, it will be stronger than it has ever been before. As you come into His presence hungry for Him, you will recover all that's been lost. Yes, I want you to claim this period as your time of divine recovery. It's time to be revived. It's time to recover.

Recover All

As you sit in the counsel of God today, I want you to ask the Lord three questions:

1. In which areas do I need revival?
2. What should I expect to recover?
3. How should I pursue what has been lost?

We know that God is all about bringing complete restoration and victory, and He has a strategy for how He will do it. He knows the part He needs you to play. In the biblical story of David, when his enemies had taken everything from him at Ziklag, David asked the Lord, "'Shall I pursue this troop? Shall I overtake them?' And He answered him, 'Pursue, for you shall surely overtake them and without fail recover all'" (1 Samuel 30:8).

At the core of it, the revival and recovery of your vision, dream, or assignment—whether it's to start a ministry or business, write a book, or record an album—the purpose is about plundering hell to populate heaven. In your pursuit of purpose, you may have suffered all kinds of losses, rejection, abandonment, criticism, abuse, or misuse. Because of what you carry, the enemy put a target on your back. So, as you seek the Lord about what you should do next, hear Him saying to you, *Yes, go in and recover everything you've lost*. Let Him teach you how to war at this level (see Psalm 18:34) and get the spoils of every single battle you've gone through.

Sometimes we spend so much effort fighting our spiritual enemies that we forget to go in and take the spoils. But you are going to reap the reward of every challenge, every battle, and every war you have had to fight. You will see great reward come to you. Your spoils may show up as wisdom, peace, inner strength, greater dependence on God, stronger faith, perseverance, or greater stewardship.

As the Lord helps you recover what's been taken, and as He restores your heart and revives your dreams, you will enter a period of celebration. This is the third phase as you come into convocation with the Lord. You are setting yourself aside to be with the Lord during these forty days. This is consecration.

You are following the leading of His Spirit to leave the old and enter the new. This is step 2, what I'm calling the crossover. And soon, you will enter a time of great rejoicing once again.

If you can see it now through the eyes of faith, you may start the celebration early. You may find yourself rejoicing now for all that He has brought you through—both good and bad— because you know the value of the struggle. You may find yourself celebrating now for what He will do in the future, because you see the vision of the good and hopeful future that He has for you (see Jeremiah 29:11). I challenge you today to let your faith be increased and give God praise in advance for the victories He's about to win on your behalf.

The Same Yesterday, Today, and Forever

Many times, people assume that the holy convocation, or the times when God called His people to Himself, is only for the Old Testament. They may say, "That's under the law. It's not necessary now." But Jesus didn't come to do away with the *wisdom* of the law. He came to fulfill it. And because the principles of His Word stand forever, we can celebrate the spirit behind these holy times, as they still speak volumes to us today. Your time in counsel with God, seeking Him as He calls you to a new level, is necessary. Hearing the Lord well enough to follow His commands helps us live the abundant life for which Jesus gave His life.

So, take this word and go into your day with the peace of God over you and with a sense of prosperity over your life, knowing and understanding the assignment of the Lord for you. Go into your day with a spirit of consecration. You may have chosen to engage this time with a combination of fasting and prayer. Stick with the commitment you made to the Lord. When the Holy Spirit begins to pull you in, respond by following Him. Do what He directs you to do, so that you can be closely in tune with Him. This is a significant time. You want the Lord to search your heart and soul as He did with ancient Israel so that you can be cleansed and purified for what is to come.

PRAYER

Father, I say hallelujah to Your name. I give You praise and glory and honor. I thank You for everything You've done for me, for every victory You've won, for every trial You've helped me overcome. I thank You in advance for securing a future for me. Father, I'm praying that as the trumpet sounds, I will be quick to respond to the announcement of consecration that will keep my commitment to fast and pray as You download to me Your plans. As this announcement of consecration is being released, I know I am exiting one place in the spirit and entering another. I welcome Your consecration. I welcome the crossover. I welcome the celebration that will come as You revive me and help me recover all that's been lost. Cleanse me, purify me, and make me ready for what's to come. In Jesus' name, Amen.

WEEK 3

Going Higher

Exit the Realm
of the Flesh

After these things I looked, and behold, a door standing open in heaven. And the first voice which I heard was like a trumpet speaking with me, saying, "Come up here, and I will show you things which must take place after this."

—Revelation 4:1

We are in a day when the Lord is unlocking the eyes of His seers. Some of us have been spiritually blind. Our discernment has been dulled. We've not seen as we should in the Spirit. But the Lord is clearing up and correcting our spiritual vision. And so, as we read our verse for today, we see that the prophet was able to look and see an open door in heaven. He was also able to hear a trumpet-like voice telling him to come up higher.

There is so much revelation in this verse, and I will share it later this week. For now, I want you to settle that your spiritual senses—your hearing and your seeing—must be keen to the

Spirit of God and to what's going on in heaven so that you can bring all God has for you down to earth. You want to be able to know when He gives direction for your life—when to come and when to go, when to be still, when to take action, when to speak, and when to be silent.

In this time of resetting and realigning, I believe we need to hear God speaking that it is time to turn the page and enter a new chapter. This is not just a new season. We've heard prophecies about seasons over and over. I've even used that expression during these forty days. But what I am sharing here is not only that. What I want you to embrace during this reset is that we are also stepping over into a new chapter. And, as we do, what the Lord is instructing us to do and what the Holy Spirit is beckoning us to do is to come up to a higher place.

This means that the Lord is challenging us to come higher as it relates to our relationship with Him. He is calling us to a higher place in our prayer life. And, while this is not really popular to say and though it is not one of those words people clamor for, you need to understand this, too: Whenever the Lord says, *Come up higher*, what He's saying is, *I'm calling you out of the realm of the flesh and into a deeper place in the spirit.* Again, this means that our prayer life must increase. We are going to have to come up higher in our dedication and consecration to the Father.

This higher place requires another level of sacrifice. It requires us to die to our flesh in order to pick up the assignment and the agenda of God. This is not a popular message, but I don't care because this is the word of God. He's calling us to a higher place.

There are assignments that perhaps we have not yet walked into because we've been walking too low. We've been walking in low-level frequencies, and we've not been able to pick up the agenda and the assignment of the Lord.

Take a moment to check your heart. Is this you? If you feel the conviction of the Holy Spirit, I want you to begin to respond to God's message to you today and come up higher.

PRAYER

Father, I hear You calling me to come up higher, and I give You my yes. I desire to be in Your presence, to walk with You as the prophets of old did. I put away the things of the flesh and commit to walking according to the leading of Your Spirit. Unlock my eyes so that I may see what You have for me. Open my ears so that I may hear Your voice. Sharpen my discernment so that I may know what things You've stored in heaven for me and Your people. In Jesus' name, Amen.

Look through
the Open Door

After these things I looked, and behold, a door standing open in heaven. And the first voice which I heard was like a trumpet speaking with me, saying, "Come up here, and I will show you things which must take place after this."

—Revelation 4:1

Today I want you to hear the Lord saying, *Come up higher, because there are things I want to show you.* Again, Revelation 4:1 speaks of an open door in heaven and of a trumpet-like voice beckoning the author to come up through it in order to see things that will take place in the future. This verse provides a picture of what it can be like as we are taken by the Spirit into the prophetic dimension. This dimension deals with what God is saying and doing.

The Holy Spirit is just as active now as He was during the book of Acts. He is moving upon the face of the earth searching for those to whom He can reveal the many things God wants us to know concerning the future. But we are going to have to come up higher in order to catch a glimpse of what that is.

If you study the Holy Spirit through the context of the New Testament, you will find that the Holy Spirit is connected to the future, and He is constantly sharing God's thoughts, plans, and agendas for what is to come. If you're one who operates in the prophetic as I do, people may ask you, "Why are you releasing a prophetic word?" It's because the prophetic ministry, in conjunction with the other fivefold ministries, is the life or the breath of the Church. It is the voice of God speaking to us. Pure and authentic prophetic ministry is the mind of God being communicated to His people. It is not the mixing that we are seeing happen today, even in the Church with division, necromancy, witchcraft, crystals, and horoscopes.

The Lord desires to communicate His heart, and the Holy Spirit is concerned about your future. He's concerned about my future. He cares about us being equipped and ready for what's coming next. This why He has placed people in the earth who can hear from Him and speak boldly on His behalf.

A New Message and Assignment

As you come into counsel with God and as He calls you higher, your life may begin to look different. Going higher in God means transformation. It means stepping into new phases of life and having new wineskins filled with new wine (see Mark 2:18–22). Your old life cannot accommodate the new things God wants to do for you and through you. This is what He said to me: *You will be stepping into another phase of your life. There are some assignments that are about to completely come to an end for you.* You may have already begun to experience this. You may have this sense that you are about to go on a new journey in which you will pick up new assignments in the Spirit. This may mean your ministry, business, profession, or other area of competency is about to shift. This may also mean that your message is about to shift.

The Lord is going to give you a new message. You are going to begin to speak new things to different crowds and deal with new spheres of influence. You're going to have a new type of assignment. You may be serving your community, family, employer, or local church. You have been on assignment, but the Lord will begin to shift how you serve in those spaces.

You are going to receive a different kind of mandate that you will pick up and begin to walk in. It will be a new assignment of the Lord. The Lord is going to thrust you into a new phase of life where those promises the Lord had given you that had become dormant are going to be revived.

You may not have seen them happen at your current level or in your current assignment. You have been waiting for them to manifest, but they have not come to pass. But as you look courageously through the door that stands open in heaven before you, you will see that the promises of God are beginning to unfold for you. The next chapter for you will be a new phase of life. You have completed some assignments, so it's time for you to shift and walk into new assignments with a new message. Let the Lord adjust your voice, for you will begin to speak the things God has called you up in the heavenlies to witness in a different way. Trust right now that it is happening for you.

PRAYER

Father, I pray that by Your Spirit I will be made worthy of the call to come up higher. I desire to know Your heart and the plans You have for my future. Empower me with the faith to see into the open door of heaven how I may be of service to You and Your people as You turn the pages of my life to a new chapter. I willingly accept the new message and mandate You've called me to in this hour. In Jesus' name, Amen.

Purify Your
Prophetic Flow

Then one of the seraphim flew to me, having in his hand a live coal which he had taken with the tongs from the altar. And he touched my mouth with it, and said: "Behold, this has touched your lips; your iniquity is taken away, and your sin purged."

—Isaiah 6:6–7

Who may ascend into the hill of the LORD? Or who may stand in His holy place? He who has clean hands and a pure heart, who has not lifted up his soul to an idol, nor sworn deceitfully.

—Psalm 24:3–4

God wants to put a new message in your mouth so that you can release to His people the mysteries of His Kingdom. There are, however, those who would want to pervert the prophetic ministry. They want to adjust the process of discerning their future in a way that better suits their agendas. You may know believers who consult psychics, witches, or mediums because they may be ignorant of God's ways concerning how He desires to speak to us. They may not be willing to wait on God, or they may have had a negative experience with prophetic ministry that sent them seeking other ways to satisfy their desire to know more about what's to come.

One of the reasons we are seeing people in the Body of Christ think it's okay to be a Christian and to consult with a medium is because we have allowed that kind of behavior in the Church. In our churches, there are people who have carried the title prophet (or other fivefold ministry title), but they have been undercover or disguised. They've operated in witchcraft, and their leaders allowed it.

We have allowed it into our organizations when we think it is okay for anyone who says they have a word from God to release it. The question becomes, which god? Or which spirit gave you that word? I've seen situations where a pastor or prophet released curses, especially in the case where someone was leaving their church. They said things like, "Well, they left my church, so everything that they do is going to fail." Some think it is all right that a minister can be upset with a person, call themselves a prophet, and release infirmity or sickness on that individual. This is witchcraft and sorcery.

We have acknowledged those kinds of individuals as prophets or apostles, but they're really operating in a spirit of sorcery. The Lord is pulling the cover off this kind of behavior. If we're going to address people in the Church who consult mediums, witches, and psychics, we're going to have to address those who call themselves prophets but are really operating in witchcraft.

We must deal with how we use our words and authority in the Body of Christ. The Bible says to "rid yourselves of all malice and all deceit, hypocrisy, envy, and slander of every kind" (1 Peter 2:1 NIV). As servants and messengers of God, we must strive to be above reproach. If we don't, we risk the heavenly words of God being mixed with the profane and destructive words of the enemy. Our words and thoughts must be acceptable to God.

When God called the prophet Isaiah, He had to purify his lips in preparation for him to speak to the people on God's behalf. Isaiah humbly knew his condition. He said, "Woe is me, for I am undone! Because I am a man of unclean lips" (Isaiah 6:5). How many prophets do you know today who would be humble enough to lay before the Lord in this way? With so many people hungry for position and status, it's hard to imagine such humility and purity of heart ruling the lives of God's chosen ones.

We must deal with our sacred cows, those things that seem too holy to change. In this instance, that means being hesitant to correct prophets who have been accurate in the past. We won't touch them because they wrote an accurate book, or they gave a large amount in the offering plate. There are so many reasons we'll overlook the witchcraft operating in the church but none of them will excuse our complicity when God comes to look at His Bride.

We are in a time where the Lord is separating the authentic from the false. He is calling us back to a place of consecration. He is reestablishing a plumb line so that we know what is pure and what is perverse. There must be a pure prophetic flow. There must be those who carry the true testimony of Jesus with the right motive and the right heart.

He's dismantling the spirit of witchcraft that has been creeping into the Church. As believers, we are not permitted by the Holy Spirit to consult with witches, psychics, or warlocks, though some of us may be tempted to turn to those sources because there is an absence of true prophetic ministry within the Church. Others of us may have shut the door to prophetic ministry because some prophets have created a bad reputation or have not operated as they should have.

There has been an absence of true prophetic ministry in the Body. People are not seeing or hearing prophetic ministry the way it was in the book of Acts. In response, they've gone to witches or consulted with psychics. They have tried to read the stars and look at the zodiac signs to know what's going to happen. True, authentic prophetic ministry is the testimony of Jesus. When it is in place, Jesus always gives us a clear picture of the future and what is coming.

He has told us about it in the Bible, and that is what we are to stand on. When true prophetic ministry is in place, we won't need to turn to a zodiac sign to tell us what's going to happen. We don't need to go to a psychic to learn about our future, because the Holy Spirit has already downloaded to us insight concerning the future.

I know you are reading this book because you want to be part of the pure things God is releasing through His people. I know you desire to see a rise of prophetic ministry. It is coming, but it will come in a different way. No longer will the prophetic be relegated to simply one or two individuals within your church or region. The Lord is saying that there is about to be a rising of companies of prophetic voices that will begin to flow in purity and will release the words of the Lord. Will you be one of them?

I believe we are going to see a new showdown between the prophets of Baal and the prophets of God (see 1 Kings 18). We are going to see a showdown between those who have operated within the false expressions of the prophetic realm and those the Lord is authentically using. God is bringing back purity to prophetic ministry. When we step out of alignment with the Holy Spirit, we become confused and begin to release confusion on others. God is clearing that up right now so that people can have clarity and understanding.

If you desire to be on the side of the prophets of God, I encourage you to submit yourself humbly before Him. Ask Him to examine your heart to search you for any impure motives or desires. Let Him purify your tongue and put a new message in your mouth.

PRAYER

Father, I lay myself humbly before You, repenting of any way that I have perverted the prophetic ministry in my life. If there have been ways that I've sought counterfeits to understand the future You have for me, I confess them now. Forgive me, Lord. Take the coal from Your altar and purify my lips. Thank You, Lord, for Your grace. Thank You for showing me where I have come out of alignment with You. Thank You for getting me back on track. I receive Your forgiveness and walk forward in confidence with You. In Jesus' name, Amen.

Access Kingdom Technology

I wisdom dwell with prudence, and find out knowledge of witty inventions.

—Proverbs 8:12 KJV

The Lord is calling you higher to give you access to Kingdom technology. We are in a period of time in which great innovation and creativity are vital to the life of the Church and its individual members. We are stepping over into a period of divine solutions. God wants to set you up as a contradiction to what we see reported in the news. Where the economy is tanking, you are going to increase. The economy may be declining, but your income may be doubling. You're stepping over into a place called innovation, a place called creativity. In this place, you will experience revelatory downloads containing divine solutions. The Lord is going to anoint your hands to begin to create and your mouth to speak words that will cause new life and momentum to surge in places that were once stalled and stagnate.

You may be in a time where you've been dealing with one problem after another. But the Lord says, *I'm calling you higher to receive answers and solutions from heaven, and you will know exactly what to do. I'm calling you higher so that you may be infused with My spirit of innovation.*

In Proverbs, the Bible talks about how the spirit of wisdom comes with witty inventions. The Lord by His Spirit is about to give you witty ideas, and witty inventions are going to be placed within your heart. You are going to dream of ideas and inventions, and when you dream of them, you will need to step out and do what you saw in your dreams.

I remember when the Lord gave me an assignment to do a particular gathering. I actually dreamed about it and saw it in detail. I had to step out in faith to do what God had revealed for me to do. The truth is that if you want the Lord to keep trusting you with mega dreams and visions, you must be faithful with the smaller ones He's already entrusted to you (see Luke 16:10). These witty ideas and inventions that God is dropping on you in this hour are downloads of the technology of the Kingdom. Through creativity and innovation, God is causing you to bring heaven to earth. He is calling you to come up higher so that He may impart to you an "as it is in heaven" anointing.

Kingdom technology is advanced far beyond the technology of this world, and we gain access to it through dreams, visions, prophecy, words of knowledge, and words of wisdom. This is why God is calling us to deepen our intimacy with Him. He shares secrets of the Kingdom with His prophets. You are not an active prophet if you can't hear from God or remain faithful in carrying out what He says. So, cultivate that time with Him in the secret place so that He can begin dealing with you in new ways through detailed pictures, strategies, and schematics.

As you enter this period of innovation, God is about to give you creative ideas and witty ideas, and inventions are going to come to you. This means that you will be met with solutions in the areas in which you have seen hard problems or where there have been issues in your community, church, or family.

I've been open about sharing how there was a time that the Lord brought me to a place in my ministry where every single system I had was operating broke because of the overload and demand. So many things were going on at once that all our systems broke down. I was actually panicking, but the Lord said to me, *Don't panic. I'm using this to expand you and your capacity to house more, to house what I'm about to release into your life.*

You're coming out of a breakdown, too, and just like God told me, get ready to receive His innovative solutions for how to expand your capacity so that you can house the greater things He will release in your life. I had to break down so that I could give you inspiration for something greater. I want you to believe this and understand that it is happening right now for you.

It is in these periods of breakdown, of shortage, that God gives creativity to His people. Through the empowering of His Spirit, we will begin to stand up with the ideas that are going to be needed for our cities, towns, and communities. We are going to have the solutions the governor is looking for.

Let's not delay doing what the Lord wants to do through us. Let's give ourselves to this time of consecration so that we may be welcomed in the secret place to hear the innovations God wants to release in the earth. Instead of accepting things as they are, let's remain expectant. Let's commit ourselves to seeking God for solutions to know how we should handle these things that are happening in the world around us.

PRAYER

Father, I pray that You would begin to cause a spirit of innovation and creativity to come upon me. I pray that You would cause revival to stir in my spirit. I pray that I will see revival not only in my community and church but also in my family. Allow me access to Kingdom technology so that I may be someone's answer they are praying for. In Jesus' name, Amen.

Feed Your
Spiritual Hunger

Do not cast me away from Your presence, and do not take Your Holy Spirit from me.

—Psalm 51:11

I am the LORD your God, who brought you out of the land of Egypt; open your mouth wide, and I will fill it.

—Psalm 81:10

At the time of this writing, the Lord showed me that we are in a decade in which we are seeing economic distress, food shortages, inflation, and high gas and energy prices. I shared many of these things in my book *Prophetic Forecast*. But I want to build on this here, because you may be going through or coming out of your own personal economic shift. You may be facing scarcity on various levels. You and those in your family or community may be facing dire circumstances.

You've come to these forty days for renewal and realignment with God's plan so that you can see a turnaround in your life or in the lives of those around you. You're hearing His call this week to come up higher, so let me encourage you. The famine, shortages, and downturns are not all that God is revealing. He also wants to help you understand the prophetic significance of the times so that you are able to walk through them with a spirit of wisdom.

I believe God wants you to know that times like you may be facing are often calling for a divine reset. As I shared in yesterday's devotion, they demand a higher level of wisdom, innovation, and creativity. There are lessons to be learned and principles to be applied as you transition through life. I want you to make it a priority to seek God for revelation on how your gift or calling can be a resource to others in challenging times. Economic downturns, famines, and cultural shifts are not supposed to make you, as a believer, want to run and hide. You are designed to be the answer. Miracles can come through your faithfulness to the visions and dreams God has given you.

It's important for us as prophetic people to stay connected to what's happening, not only in our physical world but also in the spiritual world. While God has communicated to us about physical hunger and lack of resources, there is also spiritual hunger and desperation. The Body of Christ can experience a famine of hearing His words. We see this in some of our homes, churches, and ministries. We can sense that the glory has departed, and the Spirit of the Lord is no longer there; therefore, we must come clean about our condition (see 1 John 1:9) so that we get back in a position to seek the face of the Lord. As David said, one thing we don't want is for the Lord to take our awareness of His Spirit's presence from us.

Sometimes the challenges we face in our physical world—financial lack, relationship problems, job loss, and the like—can cause us to become lax in maintaining our spiritual health. We get tired, broken, and discouraged, so we stop going after God in prayer. We may stop gathering with other believers. We may stop reading the Word. Overcome by our troubles, we may not even realize that the light of God's glory in our lives has gone out.

But I believe that even today as you meditate on these words, God is reigniting you. The Lord has given me a glimpse of the future, and He has commissioned me to begin to ignite prophetic people like you to call and commend the rain. Let the Spirit of God rain on the dry places of your life. You do understand that as prophetic people, as believers, we have been given authority over the elements—both physical and spiritual. The prophet Elijah shut the heavens and there was no rain (see 1 Kings 17). But when there was a need for it, he was able to call it forth and rain came (1 Kings 18:41–46).

I challenge you to get into God's presence and declare rain for both the natural and spiritual droughts in your life, just as Elijah did. Begin to speak over your situation that rain is coming now. You do not have to sit in your famine and accept things as they come to you. You have the ability to counter some of those things in the Spirit. Some things must be, but then there are things that we can pray about and see the hand of the Lord move. Let your faith be stirred, for those who hunger and thirst will be filled!

Take the needs of your family and community to the Lord in prayer and believe God for His divine intervention. Speak life in the midst of your drought. Get in the Word again. Come back into God's presence as you used to so that you have a word to speak that brings restoration and new life. The word of the Lord is powerful in your mouth. When you speak what God has said, you will see things begin to shift. So, open your mouth, and let Him fill it.

PRAYER

Father, in the midst of famine, in the midst of drought, and in the midst of the negative things I see going on around me, I speak forth a divine contradiction. While the economy cycles up and down, and while there may be shortages of all kinds, I pray that I respond like a tree planted by the rivers of water. Revive me again, O God. Let me be ignited so that I may be a source of nourishment in times of famine and refreshment in times of drought.

As I open my mouth, fill it with words of life so that I may see a divine turnaround in my life and in the lives of those around me. I declare that I will increase even while things look like chaos in the world. I will experience a move of Your Spirit in my life. I decree this now, in Jesus' name, Amen.

WEEK 4

Restoration Is Here

Restoring Your Faith

And the God of all grace, who called you to his eternal glory in Christ, after you have suffered a little while, will himself restore you and make you strong, firm and steadfast.

—1 Peter 5:10 NIV

Recently the Lord began to speak to me through a series of dreams. If you are a dreamer, too, then you know what it is like when the Lord wants to get a message across to you in the middle of the night. I used to dream a lot more, but now when the Lord gives me a dream, I know it's from Him, and I know He's trying to get my attention. The word He placed on my heart for you has a foundation in our verse for today, and it is this: God wants to restore you. He led me to six actions He will take to do it:

1. Building and strengthening
2. Repairing or mending
3. Completing in you what has been started

4. Equipping and preparing you for what's ahead
5. Making you who or what you should have been[1]
6. Transferring to you what you need to prosper

This week, we are going to see how each action makes up God's unique restoration plan for your life, starting with the first: building and strengthening you and your faith.

Make Me a Believer

You have come through trials. And maybe you've gone through a period in which you have had to deal with warfare. You've experienced many things in life that have caused your faith to take a hit. The Lord says, *I am restoring your faith.*

God wants me to speak to your faith today. And it's not that you don't have faith, but your faith now must go to another level. You must make sure that your faith is firm in Christ and that you are rooted and grounded in God. You must make sure that you do not waver when things come and the enemy tries to attack, or when you receive a no and God has already said yes. God wants you remain steadfast and not waver in your faith.

There are times in our walk with God that we go through the motions. We go to church because we're used to going. We lift our hands. We sing. We do all of those wonderful things. But there are moments when even as we sing and lift our hands—we may even be the one delivering the word—our faith is really under attack, or it seems really small.

We have all been there. I want you to know, however, that God is not going to leave you there. He wants to strengthen you and have you excited about Him and what He is doing in your life. Know that the strength of the Lord is coming back into you. God is going to renovate your belief system so that you won't just be another Christian—you'll be a believer.

There are many who proclaim Christianity who do not fully believe in the Word of God. But He has so much more for us than mere Christianity. He wants us to transition from being marginal Christians into a place with Him where we understand that we are believers. He wants us to be able to stand in the face of adversity, and say, "Lord, I believe Your word!" He wants us to believe what He said even when it doesn't feel as if it will happen, when we don't see a breakthrough in the natural, and when situations aren't lining up with what we expected. He wants us to stand firm and declare, "God, I am still holding onto Your word!"

To help you increase your faith, God is bringing you through His restoration process. It will come on you suddenly. Even as you are reading today's devotion, your eyes are beginning to sharpen, and God is showing you areas where your faith has diminished. Maybe you've never inspected the level of your faith or looked at where you are spiritually. Don't be discouraged by what you see, because the Lord will take you from where you are and cause your faith to rise to another level. You are going to grow from faith to faith. It is the plan and the will of God that you move from one level of faith to the next level of faith. You cannot afford to be stagnant or stuck when the Lord is calling you to a higher place.

As you come out of this time of consecration, you will be in a new place. Each time the Lord gives you a new assignment and mandate, new instructions come. This new place requires another level of faith. Your faith must be strong enough to support the higher calling. If your faith stays at level one but the Lord is bringing you to a level five or level ten anointing, then something will be missing. You will need more faith. So, this is where you can make the declaration: "Lord, increase my faith." Yes, you can ask Him for it, and He hears you and will do it.

Strength for Your Spirit

God is not only building and strengthening your faith, but He is also adding strength to your spirit. If you've been feeling spiritually weak and your prayers sound something like, "God, I don't even know if I can take the next step in front of me," then I'm speaking to you. Your spirit needs an infusion of God's strength. As He restores you, He will fortify and strengthen your spirit. You will wake up one day with courage that didn't come from you. It will be only by the Spirit of the Lord.

One of the functions and assignments of the Holy Spirit, the greatest gift we could ever receive, is to bring us strength. The Holy Spirit is a Person who walks with us everywhere we go if we would receive Him. He brings comfort, and He empowers us in our inner man. Will you open yourself up and yield to Him? Let Him fill you afresh today. Let Him give you new tongues to speak, a new prayer language.

From the inside out, He is going to empower you, and you will be strengthened even in the times of temptation. Yes, restoration comes even with this kind of strength. You will receive strength for the trials that are ahead of you. Whatever life throws at you, you will not be in it alone. The Holy Spirit will be right there empowering you and strengthening you. It's happening even as you are reading these words. Be strengthened now.

PRAYER

Oh, Lord, I receive Your call to move from mere Christianity to becoming a true believer. I want to walk in all that You have destined for me. Build and strengthen me by Your Spirit so that I may withstand the storms of life. I open myself to You. I yield to Your will. My life is Yours. Fill me afresh today. I receive a new level of faith for the new things You have for me. In Jesus' name, Amen.

Restoring Your Soul

The LORD is my shepherd; I shall not want. He makes me to lie down in green pastures; He leads me beside the still waters. He restores my soul.

—Psalm 23:1–3

We learned yesterday that God wants to retore us to Himself, and we looked at how He does this by strengthening our faith and our spirit. Today, we are going to see how God wants to restore us by repairing or mending what has been broken in our mind, will, and emotions that comprise our soul.

You might be the strong one in your group of friends or at work, or maybe you're the anointed one at church who is skilled or gifted in wisdom or prayer. You might look back and find that you've had to be strong for many others. You're the one who intercedes and stands in the gap for others, and now you've come to a place where you're in need of restoring and repair. If you are used to being strong for others, you may find it difficult to be in a place where you now need strength. That's not a bad place to be, because God's power is made perfect in weakness. Like the apostle Paul, you can say, "I will boast all the more gladly about my weaknesses, so that Christ's power may rest on me" (2 Corinthians 12:9 NIV).

It is God who makes you strong for others; however, He also calls you to rest in Him so that you can be mended and repaired from the ups and downs of life. You are there for others. Let Him be there for you. Call out to Him. Say, "Lord, now I'm in need. Will You repair me?"

I believe that with this sincere prayer, He is beginning the process of restoring your soul. He's mending what has been broken in your soul, spirit, heart, and mind. The Lord is now repairing you. As He does, don't be discouraged if it feels as if others are ahead of you and you're still stuck in a mending state. It's very important that you don't compare yourself to others. If the Lord has you in a place of mending, that's exactly where you need to be.

As your faith is repaired and your soul is restored, your trust in God is now going to come to another level. You are about to level up. This leveling up will come through God's restoration in your life. I heard the Lord say so clearly, *Tell the people I'm restoring them.* He brought this word to me in a series of dreams, and so that's what I'm telling you right now: God is restoring you. These next several months are going to be months of restoration. God will make you whole.

PRAYER

Lord, I am calling out to You today. I need Your supernatural repair. Heal my heart, mind, will, and emotions.

Restore my soul. As You bring full restoration to me, I know I am right where I'm supposed to be. I will not compare myself to others or rush the process. Do in me what You need to do so that I may be ready for what You have for me. Thank You, God, for Your healing and restoring power. Thank You for making me whole. In Jesus' name, Amen.

Restoring Your Vision

Being confident of this very thing, that He who has begun a good work in you will complete it until the day of Jesus Christ.

—Philippians 1:6

At some point in your life, the Lord gave you a vision or dream. How is that vision or dream progressing? Are you moving forward in it, or are you feeling stuck? Wherever you are on the journey to accomplishing the dream or manifesting the vision, you will at times feel that the environment surrounding your dream feels stagnate. You as the dreamer or visionary may even feel stuck. If you are in this position today, I want you to know that God has a plan to restore your vision or dream. Restoration in this context looks like completion. You may want to stop and shout right there. As we learned on Day 16, restoration includes bringing something to completion. So, you can trust that when God starts a thing in you, He is going to complete the thing He started.

If you are carrying a vision or an assignment in your spirit, or if there's something in you that you know is from God—you didn't make it up, you didn't give it to yourself, you didn't conjure it up, but you know it is a vision from the Lord—then hear by the Spirit that the Lord says, *I'm going to complete the thing I started in you. I'm going to help you take it all the way to the end.*

There is a finisher's anointing that is being released to you right now. It's an anointing for you to finish the things you have started. Your finishing will be God's restoration demonstrated in your life. You may be stuck in the middle of an assignment, a process, or a vision. God spoke something to you, and you've only seen part of it come to pass. Understand that when God says, *I'm going to restore you*, He's saying, *I'm going to complete everything I told you. I will bring it to pass.*

Do you understand that our God is not in the business of doing partial miracles? He's not in the business of delivering a partial prophecy. He doesn't give you a word but then only bring part of it to pass. Know that when God gives you a word, He is obligated to fulfill the word He spoke as long as you are in alignment with His will and purpose for your life. I want you to ask the Lord to reveal any place in your life that needs to come back into alignment with His plan for you. You are in the midst of this forty-day reset where anything that will prohibit you from moving to the next level with God needs to be exposed and then realigned—or cast out altogether. Nothing must stand in your way.

God didn't give you that ministry for you to abort it. He didn't give you that assignment for you to stop. You may be in a place where you've almost given up. You may be thinking about walking away from it all. "I'm just going to close everything up," you say. "I've given it everything I had." But this is the position God wants you in, because this is now where He can step in and carry the rest.

Unless the Lord has commanded you to make a divine shift or pivot, it is not time for you to close. It is not time for you to stop. This is the time for you to let God be God. It's the time for you to say, "God, I surrender to You in this area, and I know You will restore the vision back to me. It will come to pass."

God is going to breathe on you again. You may not, however, feel the same anointing you once did. You know there's a call on your life, but the fire has died down. There have been seasons in my life when I didn't feel anointed. I didn't feel as if God wanted to use me. Yet, it was in those moments where He used me more than He had ever used me before. Out of those moments came so many testimonies.

I remember getting ready to preach in a service. I was depressed because I had been praying for someone, and what I had been praying for in his life didn't happen. I was at a point where I said, "God, I don't feel like ministering. I don't feel like preaching today. I don't feel like doing any of it. But I will obey You because You gave me the assignment." I stood on that platform. There were hundreds and hundreds of people there. As I began to minister, an amazing breakout of healing took place. Deaf ears opened. People with notable injuries were healed instantly. People who had been in accidents were healed. There were so many miracles that we couldn't even capture all the testimonies. Though this was some time ago, I've seen this happen over and over again.

The Lord has said, *At the point when you are at your lowest, that is when I'm going to take over.* When you feel you are not anointed or that you don't have it, that is when God says,

You are right where I want you. Now, My power can be made perfect in you.

You can't sustain a ministry, grow a business, or serve your community in your own might and strength. It is only by the strength of God, and He's saying that you are about to get your anointing back. You're not getting it back like that time you felt the anointing so strong in 1995, or that other time in 2018. No, you are about to level up to another place in the anointing. God is about to anoint you afresh. Even if you did give up or even backslid, as you repent and come back to God, He will restore your vision. Your anointing is coming back, and with God, you will finish what you've started.

PRAYER

Thank You, God, for Your faithfulness to complete the work You have begun in me. The road does get long sometimes, and I do get weary. I thank You for Your restoration that comes to me looking like completion. I can't do it on my own. Thank You for walking with me through it all. In Jesus' name, Amen.

Restoring Your Future

Now may the God of peace . . . equip you with everything good for doing his will, and may he work in us what is pleasing to him, through Jesus Christ.

—Hebrews 13:20–21 NIV

When God restores you, He prepares and equips you, and He furnishes you with everything you'll need for your new assignment, the new chapter in life. This is why He called the fivefold ministry gifts: apostles, prophets, pastors, teachers, and evangelists. The Bible says they are for the perfecting or equipping of the church (see Ephesians 4:11–12). So when the Lord speaks about sudden restoration coming on you, what He is in essence saying is, *I'm going to equip you for what is ahead*.

There are times in your life where you may feel as if you are spiritually exposed or uncovered. There may also be moments in your life when it feels as though you don't have what you need for the assignment you've been called to. Resources, support, and help seem limited. Then there may be other moments in your life where you don't really feel ready—you lack experience, expertise, or education.

When the Lord says that He is restoring you, in addition to strengthening you, repairing you, and completing what has been started in you, He is also equipping you for what is ahead. So, as you realign with Him and His plans for your life, get ready to receive the equipping of the Holy Spirit. Get ready for God to begin your season of preparation so that you will be ready for every opportunity, every open door, and every assignment into which you will step. Walk in the authority and confidence of God knowing that you have been fully equipped for the thing God has for you. You'll even be equipped for the thing you need before you know that you need it. When God equips you, you are full and complete, nothing missing, nothing lacking, nothing broken.

God's equipping also comes with provision because you may be carrying a great vision—something much bigger than yourself. What God has placed in your spirit may be far beyond your budget. But hear the Lord say, *I'm going to provide for you. I've already put the resources in place. Before you get to the point of needing the resources, they're going to come.* This is the equipping of God for you.

PRAYER

Lord, I receive Your equipping. Resource me with whatever I need to accomplish all that You have for my life. I thank You in advance for provision for the assignment because it is bigger than me. But with You, I know I can do it. In Jesus' name, Amen.

Restoring You

I will restore to you the years that the swarming locust has eaten.
—Joel 2:25

It's time for you to come back to who you are. Like the prodigal son who went away, wasted all his inheritance but came to his senses, it's time for you to return. You are not only to return to who you are, but you are to return back to your place in God's family. For too long, the enemy has tried to get you off track. God knows and sees you. He knows where you went off track. He knows by your decisions, your lusts, and your flesh that you have gotten off track, but He wants to restore you and make you what you should already be. As we discovered on the first day of this week, the word *restore* means to make you what you should have been, to return you to your original purpose.

In the parable of the prodigal son, the Bible says that when the son came to himself, he repented to heaven (see Luke 15:18). Why did he repent to heaven? He had to repent to the place from where his purpose originated. He had to repent to the place from where his assignment came. Heaven knows your original design. Heaven knows God's original plans and purposes for your life. So, as you come back to yourself, God is going to restore you to your original settings. He is going to push the reset button and restore you back to where you should have been. You're coming back to the place of your purpose God designed for you before the foundation of the world, before He formed you in your mother's womb.

Say this aloud with me right now, "I'm coming back to myself."

As the author of Hebrews told the Church in his day, "For though by this time you ought to be teachers, you need someone to teach you . . . and you have come to need milk and not solid food" (Hebrews 5:12). You should have been ministering at a higher level by now, but you are in need of somebody to minister to you. This is where God's restoration comes in and gets you back to where you should have been. All it takes is for you to decide to yield to the Holy Ghost.

Restoration can come instantly. It doesn't have to take five or ten years. Unless He has said otherwise, your restoration does not require a forty-day fast. God operates outside the confines of time. He is not subject to our timetable. He does what He does in His time. So, if He says, "Be restored!" instantly everything lines up as He commands. If He says, "It's coming," then there's going to be a sudden restoration upon your life. Even now, it's happening. You are hearing the Father calling you to come back to your original purpose. You have drifted away from it, but it's time for you to come back.

Restoration, especially in terms of equipping and preparation, means to transfer something onto an individual. When the Lord restores you, He brings you into a place of transfer. He says, *Tell the people I'm bringing them from transition to transfer.*

You may have been in transition but are not stuck in a certain place or phase in the process. God is now bringing you to a place of transfer where He will not only transfer to you what you need to become who you should have been, but He will also transfer to you what you should have already had. When God brings you into restoration, you begin to experience a Joel 2:25 season. He restores to you the years the locust ate, the years that were taken from you. He's going to bring you into one of the greatest transfers you've ever experienced.

When God causes you to step into a season called transfer, you will experience restoration. Name what you need and declare, "This is the season of my life called transfer." Yes, God is going to take from one place and give you something that you did not already have. And it's not going to be restored in the same measure it was taken. No, the Lord is going to cause what you have lost to be transferred back to you in multiples. What you have lost is coming back to you one-thousand-fold. It's coming back to you multiplied, pressed down, shaken together, and running over (see Luke 6:38).

Get ready to experience abundance in your life. Restoration is abundance, but it comes through the doorway of repentance. If you are in a place right now where you're saying, "Lord, I know I should be there, but I'm stuck here," take a moment and repent. Would you pray this prayer with me now?

PRAYER

Lord, I repent. Please forgive me. I come to You now with an open and humble heart asking for restoration. You said that You would do it. Cause me to level up in every area of my life. In Jesus' name, Amen. It is so.

WEEK 5

Reset for a Relaunch

Rediscovering Your Original Purpose

The LORD has made everything for its purpose, even the wicked for the day of trouble.

—Proverbs 16:4 ESV

The word *purpose* is defined as "why you do something or why something exists."[1] In the Christian community, we often refer to it as a calling. Paul says, "I press toward the mark for the prize of the high calling of God in Christ Jesus" (Philippians 3:14 KJV). He points us to the fact that there is a high calling that we have in Christ. We were made for a greater purpose than what we may be initially aware of.

In my experience, purpose is often hidden from the one who possesses it. Most people do not become acutely aware of their purpose until they have lived through years of their lives. When I travel and preach around the country and the world, I am often asked, "How do I identify my gift or calling?" People are often unsure about what they should be doing or what gifts they have. Here are reasons your calling or purpose may be hidden:

1. It is for your protection.
2. It is because you are underdeveloped.
3. It is because you have not yet reached your destination.
4. It is not yet the time for it to be fully revealed.
5. It is because your purpose is greater than what those around you can handle.
6. It is because there is a deliverer's anointing in you that is yet to come forth.

It is important to note that God does not hide your purpose because He is being cruel. God hides your purpose as a means of protecting that which is valuable. If certain people knew your purpose and who you really are, they would try to interfere or put their hands on your gift to benefit from it.

He will hide your purpose to keep it from being contaminated. At the right time, He will cause your purpose to unfold. A part of our faith journey is about discovering—no, rediscovering—our purpose. I say rediscovering because Jeremiah 1:5 says, "Before I formed you in the womb I knew you; before you were born I sanctified you; I ordained you a prophet to the nations." The Hebrew word for *know* in that verse means "to make oneself known or to know by experience."[2] It is the depiction of both parties knowing one another and being deeply connected.

I believe that your spirit, which is eternal, already knew God before you arrived on earth. This life is about finding out what your spirit already knew—what was lost with the Fall of Adam. Through Jesus Christ's finished work on the cross, we can recover what was lost and walk in the fullness of our calling in Him.

You Rediscover Your Purpose by Discovering Who God Is

You can rediscover your purpose by being aware that you were made in the image and likeness of God. In Genesis, we hear a part of a council meeting in heaven. The early Church believed that there is a heavenly council that deliberates on matters concerning the earth. This concept is supported from Old Testament to New Testament. Genesis 1:26 states, "Then God said, 'Let Us make man in Our image, according to Our likeness; let them have dominion.'"

Humanity is the only creation known that is made in the image and likeness of God. This means you have His image—resemblance, form, and essence. You were also originally made in His likeness, that is His fashion, character, and attributes. When sin entered the world, it stripped humanity of the likeness (character) while maintaining the image (form). The book of Timothy calls it having a form of godliness but denying the inner working power (see 2 Timothy 3:5).

When we read the Word of God and allow His power to work in us, we become more like Jesus. Our character is transformed, and our hearts are made new. The more we find out who He is and what He is like, the more we understand our purpose and who we are.

Your Purpose is Revealed Through Fire

"Each one's work will become clear; for the Day will declare it, because it will be revealed by fire; and the fire will test each one's work" (1 Corinthians 3:13). Your purpose is also known as your life's work. It is the thing that you were created to do. The

Bible indicates that every person's work will be made manifest or revealed by fire. Fire is symbolic of trials, tests, and heated situations. This means that life's trials and tests have a way of activating what God has placed on the inside of you.

Some people assume that they will be told what their purpose is in church or in a spiritual setting. Church services are amazing experiences where we can get fed the Word of God and have fellowship with brothers and sisters in Christ. It gives us the tools to apply and understand God's will and word. But it is often not the setting where your purpose is awakened. More often, a test will arise within your everyday life that will bring out who God has called you to be. Embrace the fire of God. Allow Him to make manifest your purpose so that you may fully understand and walk in your calling.

PRAYER

Father, help me to embrace Your Holy Spirit fire that burns through trials and tests in order to perfect my character and reveal the purpose You have for me. I pray that You would help me to know You deeper, to experience You fully, and to be transformed to be more like You. In doing so, help me to rediscover my purpose to bring You glory. In Jesus' name, Amen.

Sharpening Your Spiritual Gifts

Therefore I remind you to stir up the gift of God which is in you through the laying on of my hands.

—2 Timothy 1:6

Every person has inherent, natural gifts. These natural gifts are talents, skills, abilities, and other things of special value. Natural gifts are empowered by mental faculties, work, and practice. But spiritual gifts come only from the Holy Spirit. Spiritual gifts have connection with the spiritual world. They are empowered by the Holy Spirit and directly affect this natural world. These gifts may also be known as:

- Endowment—capacity or power placed on someone by a higher authority
- Charisma—from the Greek word for *favor*, a gift or grace bestowed upon a person

- Miraculous faculty—defying earthly laws and protocols to serve others
- Supernatural force—divine power, might, vigor, and influence
- Spiritual ability—eternal access that enables one to accomplish work

Every Spirit-filled believer has access to all nine gifts of the Spirit. Each spiritual gift has a corresponding fruit of the Spirit (see Galatians 5:22–23). By exercising the gifts and fruit together, our spiritual ability is enhanced, and our gifts are sharpened. Spiritual gifts must be backed by godly character for them to function at their optional level. Your integrity and character matter more than your gifting does. They provide the foundation for the gifts to grow and develop. Without spiritual fruit, gifts are meaningless. Below I'll list the gift of the Spirit with the corresponding fruit that is assigned to it:

1. Wisdom—This gift works in connection with the fruit of *self-control*. It takes self-control or discipline to apply wisdom from the Spirit. The flesh will want to do the opposite of wisdom. Whether receiving from or giving wisdom, self-control is needed. The one receiving wisdom must apply it, and the one giving wisdom must practice what he or she preaches.

2. Knowledge—The fruit of *meekness* (humility) is needed to enhance the gift of knowledge. The Bible explains that knowledge puffs up (see 1 Corinthians 8:1). It is easy to become prideful when you're given supernatural knowledge of situations, people, or events.

Humility or meekness will keep you humble so that you will be able to flow in this gift. Recognizing that God is the true source of all spiritual gifts is key.

3. Faith—The fruit that balances faith is *patience*. Scripture tells us that faith develops patience (see James 1:3). Patience comes from a Greek word, *hupomone*, meaning "consistency."[3] Being consistent is remaining faithful to your commitment while you wait for the promise from God to manifest.

4. Healing—Healing flows from *kindness*, also defined as compassion. Matthew 9:35–36 says that Jesus was moved with compassion when He healed the sick. In order to allow the gifts of healing to flow, the fruit of kindness must be active in the life of the person ministering. Kindness is simply caring for others.

5. Working of miracles—Miracles come from the glory of God. One of the synonyms of *glory* in Old Testament is *goodness*. Goodness is a fruit of the Spirit, and I believe God's goodness is the atmosphere in which miracles can occur. In Exodus 33:18–23, Moses asked God to show him His glory (goodness). This should be our prayer when we ask God to use us to work miracles.

6. Prophecy—1 Corinthians 13:2 informs us that there is no need to prophesy without *love*. Prophecy is foretelling the future. When God gives us insight of the future, it is because He loves us so much that He wants us to be prepared, equipped, and encouraged. When we minister in prophecy, the fruit of love has to be the driving force.

7. Discerning of spirits—Discerning spirits requires *longsuffering*. Longsuffering is being willing to deal with

the hardship of a person or circumstance until he or she is delivered or free. God gives us this gift to discern between the spirit and the soul. The soul can have emotional trauma that requires longsuffering until wholeness occurs.

8. Different kinds of tongues—The Bible connects *faith* to praying in the Holy Spirit. "Building yourselves up on your most holy faith, praying in the Holy Spirit" (Jude 1:20). Faith is built when you pray in tongues. As well, it takes faith to pray in an unknown tongue.

9. Interpretation of tongues—*Peace* is clarity and soundness of mind. Jesus says, "Peace I leave with you" (John 14:27). This level of soundness is needed for the gift of interpretation to flow unhindered by the mind's soulish realm. Communicating and interpreting the will of God can only come through the language of peace.

Further, spiritual gifts are enhanced through the discipline of prayer, the study of the Word, and the application of biblical principles. Gifts are also sharpened by stirring them up (see 2 Timothy 1:6). Stirring your gifts is activating them by prayer and using them for the purpose of serving others. Here are attributes of your God-given gifts. Your gifts have the power to:

- Mature, grow, and develop
- Build others up in their faith
- Accelerate the promises of God by declaring His Word over the lives of others
- Bless others through supernatural power
- Add value to others through service

As your gifts are sharpened, you will be empowered to sharpen, encourage, and enhance others. Remember that you were called and given spiritual gifts to be a light in a dark world and to point people to Christ with every opportunity you have.

PRAYER

Lord, help me to fully surrender my natural gifts and talents to You so that I may pick up Your divine, spiritual gifts. Empower me to serve others with Your Holy Spirit power to affect positive change in the world. Endow me with Your power so that I might demonstrate Christ's love to those to whom I'm assigned. In Jesus' name, Amen.

Hearing the Voice of God

Man shall not live by bread alone, but by every word that proceeds from the mouth of God.

—Matthew 4:4

God is still speaking today, and He desires to have a real, personal relationship with you. There are many things within society that are aggressively fighting for our attention: entertainment, music, news—you name it. Everything in our world that is transmitting a signal is vying for our time and focus. This can make it more challenging to clear away the clutter and get to know the person of the Holy Spirit. How can you properly hear Him if everything else is so loud? "There are, it may be, so many kinds of languages in the world, and none of them is without significance" (1 Corinthians 14:10). The New Century Version translates that verse as, "There are all kinds of sounds in the world." Each sound or voice means and transmits something to the hearer. The voice of God is the most important voice, far exceeding in significance above the rest. Often, however, it is the least heard sound.

How do we learn or relearn to identify the voice of God? By spending time getting to know Him through His written Word. The more you take time with a person, the more you will get to know his or her personality, thoughts, and character. It's important that you not look at God as this distant, overlooking judge. You should see Him as Spirit, a person, someone who wants to be your closest friend. John 4:24 says, "God is [a] Spirit." In order for us to fully know Him, we must worship Him in spirit and truth. That is heart-to-heart expression without artificiality.

To know God and to know His voice, you must identify the other voices competing for attention. These voices come through desire and want. Four desires (four voices) are in front of you, and you must distinguish which is the voice of God.

1. Self-desire—This is what you or your flesh (body and soul) wants. It, most often, is against what God wants for you. It is from human desire that the voice of the soul emerges. There are times that people pray and ask God for something, but their minds have already been made up as to what He should say. So then, their soul tells them what they want to hear and mimics the voice of God. You must be careful that you are not led by your heart, will, and desire. It's important to acknowledge what you want, then line it up to the Word of God to examine your desire.

2. Misguided desire—This is what your family, friends, or others may desire for you. Now, of course, friends

and family may desire right things for your life, but I'm speaking of this in a general sense. Every person around you may have an opinion, desire, or way that seems right to them for you. Although we are to cherish our loved ones, we don't put their voice above the voice of God (written Word or the Spirit speaking to your heart).

3. Evil desire—This is the desire that your enemy wants for you. Ephesians 6:12 says, "For we do not wrestle against flesh and blood." Our fight is with demonic spirits fueled by evil Satan and his agenda. Evil spirits, also known as familiar spirits, devils, or unclean spirits, speak to people if there is an open door of opportunity. The word devil comes from the Greek word *diabalos*, meaning "to throw slander."[4] He often does this by little whispers in the mind. Sometimes the enemy's voice can come in the form of what you think is a thought. If it does, you must reject that demonic voice. The voice of the enemy will tell you to do something contrary to the Bible that would cause negativity or harm to yourself or others. You can silence that voice by speaking the Word of God against him.

4. Pure desire—This is what God desires for you. Pure desire is the heart, will, and mind of God being released to you. Through this vehicle, the voice of God speaks. He loves you so much that He only wants the best for you. Even if what you're experiencing doesn't feel as if it is good. The end result of God's voice to His people will always bring repentance and great things to the

hearer. The voice of God is our defense and powerful protection.

"My sheep hear My voice, and I know them, and they follow Me. And I give them eternal life, and they shall never perish; neither shall anyone snatch them out of My hand. My Father, who has given them to Me, is greater than all; and no one is able to snatch them out of My Father's hand."

John 10:27–29

God, in His love and mercy, communicates to us in many ways. The ultimate way that God speaks is through His written Word; what we call the Bible. Torah, Scripture, or His written Word is the measuring stick that we use to judge everything else. The Bible is the inerrant Word of God and should be treated as such. God then speaks to us, Spirit to spirit. He may come as a small, still voice to your heart. The more you come to know Him, the louder that voice may become. God speaks through dreams and visions, and He speaks through nature and signs in the earth. Lastly, God speaks to us through other people. Anointed and consecrated preachers—ministers of the Gospel—carry the Word of God.

In whatever mode the Lord chooses to communicate, we must have listening ears to hear Him.

PRAYER

Lord, help me to know You more deeply and more intimately. I want You to be my closest friend. It's my desire to develop a pure and real relationship with You. I pray that You would fine-tune my heart and my spiritual ears so that I can hear You. Speak to me, Father. I open my spirit to receive Your Word. I pray that I would not follow any other voice but Yours. In Jesus' name, Amen.

Launching Out

When He had stopped speaking, He said to Simon, "Launch out into the deep and let down your nets for a catch."

—Luke 5:4

Stepping out into something you've never done before can be daunting and intimidating. You know that you can't afford to stay where you are, but at the same time, you're challenged by the fear of the unknown. Launching out into the deep has become a metaphor for stepping out into uncharted territory and going beyond what you are familiar with. In the book of Luke, Peter and the others were fishing but had not caught anything. Jesus gets in the boat with them and begins teaching. After He had finished teaching, He tells them, "Launch out into the deep and let down your nets for a catch." Their reply to Him was, "We have toiled all night and caught nothing" (verse 5).

Coming Through a Night Season

It's significant to me that Scripture places emphasis on the time of day by describing that they had worked hard all night. Night is an interesting concept in Scripture. Obviously, it deals with the part of a day when the sun goes down and the moon becomes visible. It the Bible, however, night can also be symbolic of a season or period of darkness, affliction, turmoil, or limited vision. David said, "I will bless the LORD who has given me counsel; my heart also instructs me in the night seasons" (Psalm 16:7). Likewise, when Job went through devastation, he referred to it as a night season (see Job 30:17). Sometimes launching out and experiencing the great things that God has for you requires that you endure a night season. A night season can be characterized by:

- Darkness—Increased wickedness, evil, or demonic oppression
- Limited sight or vision—Unable to see spiritually, having diminished vision or lacking a clear plan, confusion
- No productivity—A lack of fruitfulness, advancement, and progression in life
- Night Terror—A spirit of fear or other form of demonic attack meant to bring spiritual paralysis
- Challenge—Difficulty, affliction, or infirmity. It could also be seen as a trial or hard situation

When Jesus stepped into the boat with Peter and the other disciples and began teaching, He was declaring an end to their night season—their season of toiling with no productivity. Likewise, as you grab onto the Word of God and obey His command to launch out, there will be an end to your night season. The disciples replied to Jesus, saying, "'Nevertheless at Your word I will let down the net.' And when they had this done, they caught a great number of fish, and their net was breaking" (Luke 5:5–6). Out of the toiling of the night season comes a launching out. After the launching out comes a net-breaking harvest.

Strategies for Launching Out

1. Wash Your Net

    When Jesus found the disciples on the shore of the lake in Luke 5, they were washing their nets. A fishing net is a tool used for catching a wide variety of fish. It's very different from simply using a fishing rod or pole. With a fishing pole, you have to use bait to catch a specific type of fish. You can only catch one at a time. A dragnet has been used for centuries by fisherman to pull in multitudes of fish. Because debris, trash, or other materials would get caught in the net, fisherman made a common practice of washing and repairing their nets so that they could be ready for the next catch. When you're preparing for an abundant harvest, you must wash and repair your net. A net is symbolic of your network—circle of friends and close people, net worth—in this case, valuable spiritual possessions.

2. Bring Jesus onto Your Ship

    One of the key elements of the story of the great catch in Luke 5 is that Jesus came to the ship before the fishermen saw any great results. This is what we are to do in every area of our lives: we must bring Jesus onto our ship. This statement signifies making Him the center in all things. When Jesus is the foundation of your life, you can never go wrong. A ship can be a prophetic symbol of a relation*ship*, a friend*ship*, wor*ship*, part-ner*ship*, fellow*ship*, pastor*ship*, workman*ship*, apostle-*ship* and more. A ship is a vessel for transporting us to a destination. We are to acknowledge and submit to the Lord*ship* of Christ. When you bring Him onto your ship, you're setting yourself up for great success. He has to become the focus of your worship, the basis of your relationships, the bedrock of your family, the motivation of your ministry, and the reason you do what you do.

3. Teaching Unlocks Your Harvest

Jesus didn't just enter the ship, He taught them while He was on it. Teaching, in many regards, is becoming a lost art. Teaching that is from the Spirit of God is an ancient tool to download insight and revelation into the heart of the receiver. Sound, solid, Bible teachers are needed to ensure the growth of believers. While it is a necessity that you study the Word of God for yourself, you still need someone who is anointed and who understands the teachings of Christ to pour into your spirit. Have you ever been familiar with a principle, and you know it works, but the minute you hear someone in the field of study show you how to apply it, it clicks in your mind? That's the power of teaching. We are not our own teachers; we need others who have a different perspective and are connected to the Father's heart to teach us. Romans 10 says, "How can they hear without a preacher?" (verse 14). The Greek word translated preacher, *kérussó*, means "a herald"[5] and can be synonymous with teacher.

Godly teaching gives you the tools that unlock your greatest harvest. When Jesus taught them, not only was it nourishing to their spirits, but I believe that it caused the environment around them to respond to the life-giving word they were receiving. It is my belief that His teaching opened the floodgates for the multitude of fish to be caught. And likewise, biblical teaching will accelerate your personal harvest.

4. Go Deeper

In so many words, Jesus told the disciples to go deeper. They had been in the shallow area of the lake. I've been at this lake in Galilee many times. I've been on boats in this exact spot that this event happened. It's breathtaking, it's ancient, and the scenery is other worldly, flooded with peace and serenity. The water gets deeper as you go out. Going deeper signifies being submersed in the things of God. God is calling us to go deeper in prayer, deeper in praise and worship, and deeper in the study of the Word. It's time to go deeper in Him. You can only rise in life to the corresponding depth of your relationship with Jesus. Whenever you get ready to launch out into any endeavor in the natural, whether it is business, career, personal, or ministry, you must make sure that it's backed with a depth of intercession and prayer.

5. The Biggest Catch of Your Life

Lastly, when the disciples launched out into the deep and obeyed the instructions of the Lord, they saw great results. They had been in the same areas toiling all night and had caught nothing. But it was at His word that they launched again. Sometimes God will require you to do what you've done before. Maybe the last time you tried, there were no results. Maybe the last time you tried, you left disappointed. This time, however, at His word, you will see a great harvest. The catch of fish was so great the Bible says they had to call for help (see Luke 5:7). Within this next chapter of your life, God is going to send assistance to you. The right people are coming who are yoked to your vision and assignment.

PRAYER

Heavenly Father, I pray that You would help me position myself for the great harvest that You are sending into my life. Strengthen me to come through my night season empowered to walk in greater purpose. Give me a stronger hunger for Your Word. Fill me afresh with Your Spirit, and take me deeper in You. I pray this in Jesus' name, Amen.

Stepping into Your Next

And He changes the times and the seasons.
—Daniel 2:21

A new chapter in your life is inevitable. You can't escape the fact that life is changing; things around you are not quite the way they used to be. People around you are changing, and relationship dynamics are shifting. If you pay close attention, you'll even notice that you are changing. Microelements of your personality that were hidden are coming to the surface. You may notice that you speak more freely—you don't hide your feelings as much. You used to be afraid of being alone and by yourself. Now, you crave that time to refuel and prepare for what is next on your agenda. Even the world looks different from what it did when you were growing up. Honestly, it looks different from what it did five years ago. So, what's happening to your world? What's happening to you? You're changing, shifting, growing, evolving, and so is everything around you. You're stepping into your next! Whether you like it or not, your next phase, your next chapter, and your next season are about to collide with your life.

God created everything to progress and change over time. It's the part of life that can bring the most trepidation because we are often creatures of habit. People don't always like change. As you grow through life, you must learn to embrace change.

A New Season

A season is a period of time that governs the earth's cycles. It is characterized by a ninety-day period. It is accompanied by specific effects in nature, in weather patterns, and the like. Spiritual seasons are quite different. A spiritual season could last for weeks, months, or possibly even years. The spiritual realm is not bound by time in the same way that the earth realm is. A spiritual season may be characterized by heaven's response to your life. There are reaping/harvest seasons, giving or sowing seasons, testing seasons, nights seasons, promotion seasons, and more.

Every new season is an opportunity to experience God in a new way. Whether you're being tried in your faith, going through a process, or reaping a reward, it's an opportunity for God to get the glory in your life.

Releasing the Old

You can't fully walk into your next until you first release the old. So many people get stuck on what God did in their lives years ago. They are paralyzed by previous victories or by traumatizing failures. The plan of the enemy is to get you so fixated on what was that you never step into what will be. Your next place in God requires a clear decision that you will not look back. You must let go of all that happened in your past, whether good or bad, in order to move into the new things of God. Jesus said, "No one, having put his hand to the plow, and looking back, is fit for the kingdom of God" (Luke 9:62).

Failures will not disqualify you from the Kingdom of God because repentance is available. Missing the mark won't disqualify you from the Kingdom of God because you can ask for forgiveness and make a better decision. The only thing that can stop you from fully entering the Kingdom of God is looking back. Looking back toward who you were before God transformed you, looking back to what you did before, looking back toward where God brought you from with a desire to go back—these are disqualifiers.

Jesus reminds us of a pertinent story. He says, "Remember Lot's wife" (Luke 17:32). Her story occurs in Genesis 19. Lot and his wife were fleeing Sodom and Gomorrah due to its culture of sin, abomination, and prideful hearts rejecting repentance. God sent word that He was going to destroy the two cities. Lot, his wife, and family were given a way to escape. The angel of the Lord told them that the only condition was that they don't look back as the cities are being destroyed.

They were fleeing the city. They were experiencing a great supernatural deliverance. "But his wife looked back behind him, and she became a pillar of salt" (verse 26). The words *looked back* is a Hebrew word meaning "to look intently, to regard with pleasure."[6] She looked back with a longing to return. Although those cities were riddled with rebellion and iniquity, she missed them. It disqualified her, and she became fossilized in that spot the moment she looked back.

There are many lessons from the story of Lot's wife. If you desire to hold on to the old thing, the old place, the old people

God brought you away from, then you, too, could become spiritually fossilized—stuck in the same emotional, spiritual, and mental place while your body ages. That's why it's so important to let go of all of the old things and allow God to make everything new. As you release the old, you will receive God's refreshing, and you will be free to step into your next.

The Next Phase

Here are some key takeaways as you step into your next phase:

- Your next phase will require boldness. Walk in the boldness and courage of the Lord. Dispel fear and take faith. "Have I not commanded you? Be strong and of good courage" (Joshua 1:9).

- Prepare for your next! Preparation is the key to embracing what God has for you. Mentally prepare by clearing your mind of old ways. Renew your mind with God's Word, and change your thinking to align with His will. Prepare your heart by setting your affections on the Lord. Prepare naturally by bringing order and organization to your personal life. Order is always the prerequisite for manifestation.

- Be willing to adapt to change. Some things in your world are about to shift so rapidly that you will feel as if you had no time to prepare. When this happens, it's easy to feel as though you are untethered and unstable. You are not! God knew that this change was coming even if you didn't. Trust in the Lord, and He will guide you. Quickly embrace the change and adjust, knowing that it will work out for the better.

- Ask God for wisdom. You're going to need it for where you're going. With every level there is a new challenge and a great reward. Wisdom will be your compass, and godly knowledge will be your sail.

PRAYER

Father, there are changes happening all around me. Prepare me for what's coming next. Help me to embrace the changing seasons and to trust in You with all my heart, mind, and soul. I pray that You would give me a plan in the midst of transition. Equip me to thrive, excel, and succeed amidst the change and bring glory to Your name. Allow me to step into my next phase with joy, excitement, divine power, and authority. In Jesus' name, Amen.

WEEK 6

Redeeming
the Time

Recovering
What Was Lost

So I will restore to you the years that the swarming locust has eaten, the crawling locust, the consuming locust, and the chewing locust, my great army which I sent among you.

—Joel 2:25

The Bible is a book about God's divine recovery plan for His people. It all started with the Fall of Adam (and Eve) in the Garden of Eden. When they fell from their place of relationship with the Father, humanity was sent into a downward spiral. They were separated from the presence of God. Over the course of time, God established a covenant with righteous men such as Noah, Abraham, and Moses as leaders or deliverers to lead His people back to Him.

People continued to rebel and reject God's loving pleas to return. Yet, God's love and mercy endured. He sent His only begotten Son who was God wrapped in flesh. He would become the sacrifice for the sin of humanity and bring restoration to all things. Jesus laid His life down, was buried in a tomb, and resurrected on the third day for the sins of the world. The finished work of the cross is God's restoration plan for humanity.

The enemy's number one job is to fight people from becoming a partaker of God's restoration plan through His Son, Jesus Christ. "The thief does not come except to steal, and to kill, and to destroy. I have come that they may have life, and that they may have it more abundantly" (John 10:10). The threefold attack of Satan is to steal, kill, and destroy. Let's look at each of these words to gain understanding of the devil's devices.

The Devil Wants to Steal from You

To steal is to take away what belongs to someone else by means of theft. A thief often searches for what is valuable to gain illegal possession of it. Likewise, the enemy is after your soul, mind, assignment, and calling because it is valuable to the Lord. You must come to the realization that you—yes, you—are valuable.

Sometimes, the enemy can try to steal your peace, joy, and dreams when you go through trauma, pain, and disappointment. For some, he uses disappointment, fear, and stagnation to steal your time. I've known many people who have experienced a severe trauma, and they are stuck in the exact year and date that the trauma occurred. A person's life could be stuck in 1998 because that's the year that the divorce occurred. A person could be at an emotional age of eleven even though she is an adult because that's the year that the abuse happened. Every time she is triggered, she becomes reduced to the age of eleven in her memories, tears, isolation, and tantrums. When you see things like this, it is a sign that a thief has entered and stolen precious goods. In this case, he's stolen time, progression, and growth. But don't be discouraged, God is a restorer.

Joel 2:25 tells us that God will restore the years that were lost in your life. No matter what you've gone through you can recover and redeem time that seemed as if it was taken from you. To restore is to bring back to its original state as if it were never harmed. To restore is to locate and recover what was lost. Supernatural restoration is God's power to put broken pieces back together. When you call upon the Lord for restoration, He will hear you, He will answer, and He will restore you!

The Devil Wants to Kill

Death, in Scripture, does not always mean extinction. Some interpretations show that it can mean separation from something.[1] When someone loses the friendship of a person that they've known for thirty years while that person is alive but is no longer in their lives, they've experienced the death of a relationship. A person can experience the death of a dream, vision, or mission. Some people feel as though their career is no longer viable.

The devil wants to cause separation and death to your God-given dreams. He wants to kill them and cause you to abort your assignment and your purpose in the earth. But the devil is a liar! He cannot kill what God has anointed to live. In place of demonic words of death, you can speak life. When you speak the words of God, life springs up. You can apply this practice to your life by reading a verse of Scripture and saying it aloud. It will combat negative words in your mind. As an example, Psalm 118:17 says, "I shall not die, but live, and declare the works of the LORD." This verse can come alive in your spirit as you confess it openly in prayer. When you speak something aloud, you are making a declaration. Your words are powerful.

Another way that the enemy tries to kill is through character assassination. He will attempt to use wounded people to kill your character in front of others so that they will not be able to receive God's expression of ministry through you. Character assassination is an age-old demonic weapon that has been used by Satan, also known as the accuser of the brethren. The Bible says, "And they overcame him by the blood of the Lamb and by the word of their testimony, and they did not love their lives to the death" (Revelation 12:11). The way that we overcome demonic assassin spirits is to apply the blood of the Lamb, Jesus Christ, to ourselves and to proclaim the testimony of salvation. Christ's salvific work has the power to overthrow the weapons of the enemy. And because you are in Him, no weapon formed against you will be able to prosper (see Isaiah 54:17).

What He Can't Kill, He Will Try to Destroy

Since the enemy can't kill your purpose, vision, or assignment from God, he will try to destroy it. The Greek word for destroy is *apollumi*. It means "to put out of the way entirely, abolish, put an end to ruin, and to render useless."[2] That is the exact intent of the enemy. He may not be able to take you out, but he is cunning in his attempt to take you off course. How does he do this? Through the temptation of sin, through the lust of the flesh, and through seeds of doubt. He ultimately wants you to veer from the course of God's Word because of unbelief. If he can get you to stop believing God, he can ruin or destroy your life.

The latter part of the definition of destroy is "to render useless." The enemy uses a cloak of religion to lull Christians into deception. Just because a person comes to church, sings about God, and even quotes Scripture verses doesn't mean that he or she is of use to the Father. Religion gives the appearance of usefulness and service to God. But it is only true relationship with the Father, through Jesus Christ, that can bring fruitfulness and true service before the Lord. To be useless is to be ineffective, unproductive, and no good for a service or task. The enemy would love for you to have the appearance of a devoted Christian but miss your purpose.

Thank God, however, for His Holy Spirit who restores us back to purpose when our lives appear to be in ruin. Thank God for His precious Holy Spirit who restores our souls when the enemy has tried his best to fracture it. He is the only one who can bring us back to His original plan for our lives. By yielding to the inner work of the Holy Spirit through His Word, you can combat the devil's plan of destruction.

You Will Recover!

I believe that you are coming into one of the greatest times of divine recovery that you've ever experienced. I detailed the tactics of the enemy, not to cause you to be fearful in any way, but to make you aware. The devil is cunning, but he is no match for our God. Restoration is a part of your spiritual inheritance. Restoration is a direct promise from God for your life.

If you've been dealing with hopelessness and thoughts that you may never see God's promise manifest in your life, rebuke the words of the enemy and tell the devil to shut up! Take faith in God's Word, get your hope back, and know that God didn't bring you this far to leave you in an unfinished state. He didn't bring you this far to drop you. "The LORD will perfect that which concerns me; Your mercy, O LORD, endures forever" (Psalm 138:8). That should be your declaration. God will perfect you. God will complete you. He will finish what He started!

PRAYER

Father, I've seen the enemy try to steal, kill, and destroy, but Your Word says in John 10:10 that Jesus came that I might have life and have it more abundantly. I pray that life, newness, fruitfulness, and abundance would spring up in me and around me. I bind the enemy's plans and weapons against my purpose. I declare that, according to Your Word, I will recover all. In Jesus' name, Amen.

Discerning Your Season

To everything there is a season, a time for every purpose under heaven.

—Ecclesiastes 3:1

Throughout this devotional, I use the word *season*, because according to Ecclesiastes 3:1, all life is governed by them. No matter where you go, you cannot escape seasons. Seasons are known as periods of time in which certain activity takes place. It is the same with spiritual seasons. They are periods of time in which certain activities occur in the spiritual realm that affect the natural realm. The Bible explains that a man who doesn't know his time is like a fish that is caught in a cruel net or like a bird that is caught in a snare (see Ecclesiastes 9:12). This is not to suggest that we must know everything that will happen in our lives—that's impossible. But understanding God's seasons for your life could help you understand why certain things are taking place in and around you.

Further, the Bible explains the types of spiritual seasons or times that a person has while they are on the earth (see Ecclesiastes

3:2–8). I have classified these 28 life cycles that govern humanity. Understanding them can help you navigate through what you may be experiencing and walk through it with grace:

1. A time to be born—This refers to the time you were born but also any other period where something new is being birthed. Birthing can happen in various times throughout a person's life—from the birth of a baby to the birth of an idea or business. These are exciting times of both pain and joy. The labor to push it out can be excruciating; nonetheless, the joy of birthing it makes it worth it. You know you're in a birthing season when something new is emerging.

2. A time to die—Death is inevitable. In Christ, it is a reward for the believer. But this season doesn't just refer to that. It refers to the end of something. Everything has both a start and an end time. The end of a relationship, career, assignment, or course can often bring grief. It can also be a period of separation. If you are in this season, you should pull close to the Holy Spirit. He is our Comforter (see John 14:26). He is always near the brokenhearted.

3. A time to plant—Planting is a time of starting something new. Farmers understand this. Planting is part of the growing process that is labor intensive. This is the time in which seed is going into the ground. It represents a season where you're nurturing something that starts small but has the potential to become great.

4. A time to pluck what is planted—This is a season of harvesting. When a crop has come to full maturation,

you reap what you've sown. I often call this a reaping season. What you've given out comes back to you.

5. A time to kill—A time to kill is not referring to physically harming someone. It is a season of severing or ending something. It can also represent a time of nourishment. In biblical times, they would sacrifice or kill an animal in order to be nourished.

6. A time to heal—This is a season to be restored, repaired, and built up.

7. A time to break down—This is a season of deconstruction. There are times during which things in your life must be broken down in order for God to reconstruct and rebuild.

8. A time to build up—This is a season in which God constructs something by putting parts or material together. Building up also means making you stronger as well as more developed and established.

9. A time to weep—Tears are unspoken prayers in liquid form. Weeping can be an expression of relief. There are tears of sadness and tears of joy. A season of weeping is an emotional period during which the soul must release what is bottled up.

10. A time to laugh—This is a season of overwhelming joy. When God places you in this season, you will laugh. Laughter is like medicine to the soul.

11. A time to mourn—This is a time of mourning, grieving, and discomfort that can be brought on by life's trials, pain, transition, or trauma.

12. A time to dance—Movement is a language. When people dance, they are moving to rhythm and

expressing excitement. This is a season of excitement, expectation, and movement.

13. A time to cast away stones—Casting away stones is a depiction of a farmer clearing away debris in order to plant. This is a season of clearing, removing, and decluttering one's life in order to start something fresh.

14. A time to gather stones—In ancient times, stones were gathered for building a house or shelter. It was a preparation period and a season of order, organization, and construction.

15. A time to embrace—To hug or embrace is to hold onto something. There are times in a person's life in which he must hold onto something. This process brings comfort, peace, and security.

16. A time to refrain from embracing—There is also a time to refrain from hugging or embracing. Spiritually, this represents a season of letting go. If you are in this time, you must release back to God what was given to you.

17. A time to gain—This is a season of increase in a person's life. When you gain, you experience addition, or even multiplication.

18. A time to lose—When you lose, you are deprived of something. You fail to gain, or you become unable to find something. Loss of any kind can be difficult. This season is at times necessary to teach us dependence upon the Lord.

19. A time to keep—To keep is to retain or maintain something. This represents a season of steady maintenance in a person's life. During this season things may be solid, balanced, or consistent.

20. A time to throw away—This is a season of pruning and purging. There are periods where cutting away is necessary to cause sustained growth in the future.

21. A time to tear—The word *tear* is also translated as "rend." It is the Hebrew word *pashach* meaning "to tear in pieces in order to make wide or large."[3] This is a season of expansion that is preceded by breaking and warfare.

22. A time to sew—Sew is the Hebrew word *taphar*, and it means "to sew or knit together."[4] God institutes this season in a person's life when He is knitting together various parts to create a whole.

23. A time to keep silent—Seasons of silence require listening to God and to those God has placed in our lives in a deeper way.

24. A time to speak—This is a season of boldness in which your voice must be heard. You cannot remain silent or hide in obscurity. Your sound must arise.

25. A time to love—Love is not just an emotion of attachment to a thing or person. Love is a covenant and a decision. When you are in this season, God is requiring a commitment for something or someone.

26. A time to hate—We must hate what God hates. Sin, missing the mark and not pleasing God, is something that we must abhor. A season of hating is about deciding for Christ and against evil.

27. A time for war—There is a time during which you must fight. Ephesians 6:12 informs us that we are not battling with flesh and blood. We must wage war against wickedness and demonic entities.

28. A time for peace—Peace is God's gift to believers. Although believers should always have peace, there are times when God will put them in a season of peace. This means there is a ceasefire to the warfare and battles in our lives as we enter a time of refreshing.

As you've explored the 28 seasons or cycles that occur throughout a person's life, examine your own life, and ask the Lord what season you are in. It's possible to experience these seasons numerous times. It's also possible that you haven't fully experienced any of them yet. You can discern your season by key identifying earmarks:

- Environment—When you are in a specific season, you don't have to make that season emerge—the environment will announce it. Think about the natural seasons. Take fall for instance. When we are in the fall season, no one has to command it or pray for it. It just comes on its own. It is announced by the cooling of the temperatures and the changing colors of the leaves. Spiritual seasons are the same. The atmosphere around you announces them. If you are experiencing overwhelming and unspeakable joy and laughter, and God's using it as medicine for your soul, then you are in the season of joy. Embrace it and take it all in because you may need those valuable deposits for your next season.

- Pattern—Seasons can be identified by patterns. Every summer, we see a pattern of signs. Temperatures rise, birds come out more, trees are in full leaf, and butterflies are fluttering all around. Every summer we will see the same patterns. It's the same when it comes to spiritual seasons. As I've listed above, when you see the patterns, you'll know the season.

PRAYER

Father, I pray that You would help me to discern and properly navigate the season that I'm in. Teach me how to rely on You and remain consistent no matter the season. Help me to be consistent in and out of season, when it feels good and when it doesn't, when I'm comfortable and when I'm uncomfortable. Teach me how to be content. In Jesus' name, Amen.

Understanding God's Timing

As the heavens are higher than the earth, so are my ways higher than your ways and my thoughts than your thoughts.

—Isaiah 55:9 NIV

The ways of the Lord often elude us. Why God allows one thing over another is beyond our human, finite understanding. In order to understand the ways of the Lord, we need His mind. As believers, the apostle Paul says, "But we have the mind of Christ [to be guided by His thoughts and purposes]" (1 Corinthians 2:16 AMP). What a powerful verse of Scripture. We can possess the mind of Christ by becoming one with Him. The more we get to know Jesus and spend time in His Word and in worship, the more we become like Him. We can pick up His heart and thoughts regarding a matter. Furthermore, we can understand the timing of God regarding a thing or situation.

The Waiting Period

When God gives you a promise, it hardly ever aligns with when you want it to happen. There is always a waiting period that you must endure. God's timing is designed to test your character. He's not just interested in making sure you get the promise or to the promised place; He's also interested in who you will have become by the time you get there. The word of the Lord over your life must test you. "Until the time that his word came to pass, the word of the LORD tested him" (Psalm 105:19). The Hebrew word used for *tested* in this verse is *tsaraph*. It is associated with the occupation of a goldsmith, and it describes one who melts down precious metals in the fire in order to refine them. It means "to smelt, refine, and test."[5] God placed Joseph in the refiner's fire.

If you've received any promise from the Lord, be prepared to be smelted through the trials of life so that you can be ready to handle it when it comes. I know that doesn't sound good. But it is good for you. God cares so much that He won't allow the fire to consume you, but He will allow it to perfect and make you ready.

"But those who wait on the LORD shall renew their strength; they shall mount up with wings like eagles, they shall run and not be weary, they shall walk and not faint" (Isaiah 40:31). Within this verse are the steps of the waiting process: waiting, mounting, running, and walking. Let's explore this further.

Waiting

The word *wait* used in the above verse has a different meaning than our English word for wait. This Hebrew word, *yachal*, means "to wait with hope or expectation; to look eagerly for."[6]

When you are waiting on the timing of God to fully manifest, you must maintain your expectations. Waiting is about a heart posture and maintaining a focus on Jesus. Waiting is about being hopeful and expectant. Waiting is the longest part of the process for manifestation. It's the most grueling part because you have to fight through doubt and fear. You have to deal with all of the *what ifs* that the enemy sends to your mind.

In spite of all of that, when you make it through and hold on to your expectation, God will perform what He said. When you wait on God, the Bible says you will renew your strength. This means that there is a blessing in the waiting. The Lord will give you supernatural strength to endure, to hold on to His promise, and to stand against demonic attacks. There is renewing that happens in your waiting!

Mount Up

Mount up means to ascend, to spring up, and to grow. This is the point in the Lord's timing in which you begin to see the budding of the flower. Things in your life begin to bloom. When you get to the beginning of manifestation, you are in an ascended place. You've passed the test of waiting, and now you will mount up with the wings of eagles.

I love studying eagles. They are some of the most fascinating birds. They use their massive wingspan to combat the wind resistance. Instead of buckling under the pressure of the wind, eagles use the resistance to propel them higher. God will cause you to do the same. After you've waited, you will use the spiritual resistance and warfare to propel you higher. Then you will receive the reward of God.

Run and Not be Weary

The spirit of weariness comes to stop you from receiving the fullness of God's promise. Galatians 6:9 says, "Let us not grow weary while doing good, for in due season we shall reap if we do not lose heart." God's assurance to you is that if you wait on His timing and go through the process, you will not be weary. Weariness can cause you to faint, but the spirit of weariness will leave your life as you submit to the waiting process of God. Scripture also says you will run. This means that you will pick up speed spiritually. Where there were delays and stagnation, you will now experience prophetic acceleration.

You Will Walk and Not Faint

Walking denotes your course in life. Wherever you go, as long as you are depending on the Father, you will have a grace that causes you not to faint. Your steps have been instrumentally ordered by God. He will align your feet with His words. This means that you will walk by faith. That's how you'll see the full manifestation of what God has said concerning you, your family, and your purpose.

PRAYER

Father, I pray that You would give me understanding of Your timing. I've tried to do things according to my plan, but it does not measure up to Your perfect ways. Teach me Your ways, show me Your plans, and help me to fully submit to Your will. I believe, and in due time, I will receive every promise that You've spoken over my life. In Jesus' name, Amen.

Times of Refreshing

Repent therefore and be converted, that your sins may be blotted out, so that times of refreshing may come from the presence of the Lord.

—Acts 3:19

Repentance is a word that we hear thrown around loosely in both Christendom and the secular world. You can jump onto social media and see someone scolding viewers, shouting at them to repent. You can enter any church service during an altar call and hear the preacher admonishing congregants or attendees to come to the altar and repent of their sins. It's a beautiful thing to witness a person truly repent and give their heart to the Lord. I've also witnessed people cry and say they are sorry, only to turn around and not change. The word repent doesn't mean saying "I'm sorry." There should be godly sorrow when we displease the Lord. That genuine sorrow leads us to repent. The word *repent* comes from the Greek word *metanoeo* and means "to change one's mind for the better, to wholeheartedly amend with abhorrence of one's past sins."[7] Repent is also associated with a militaristic term about-face. It is to turn in the opposite direction.

Any time God gets ready to take you into a deeper relation with Him, He requires another level of repentance. That means truly turning away from the past and laying aside sins and weights that could take you off course. Repentance opens the door to God's abundant blessings in your life. It opens the door to greater freedom as a believer. According to Acts 3:19, repentance is the step before conversion, which is a transformation of the heart. And that leads to times of refreshing in the presence of the Lord.

Your Refreshing is Here

As you allow the Holy Spirit to have access to your heart through true repentance, He sends winds of refreshing to you. The first wind of refreshing comes into your mind. He blows away the doubt, fear, bondage, and strongholds of the past and brings renewing. Then God refreshes your soul. Your soul is being redeemed from the intrinsic weapons of the enemy. Through the inner work of the Holy Spirit, He breathes new life into the souls of His sons and daughters. When God refreshes you, it is on purpose and for purpose. There are several key things that happen when God refreshes you:

- He empowers you—refreshing brings supernatural inspiration that enables you to do what you've been called to do.
- He invigorates you—refreshing from the Lord revitalizes and energizes you, giving you renewed strength.

- He renews you—refreshing from the Lord brings restoration. He renovates and transforms your mind to house more of Him.
- He gives you greater focus—when the refreshing of the Lord comes upon you, it enhances your spiritual eyesight. You are given an anointing to see beyond the natural into the eternal realm.
- He refuels you—refreshing from the Lord gives you a refueling so that you are able to move forward with more grace, power, and anointing from the Lord. You will be filled back up so that you may pour into others.

Angels of Refreshing

Our verse in Acts 3:19 doesn't just say that refreshing will come—it says that times (plural) of refreshing will come. I believe that God can bring you into lengthy periods of refreshing. Jesus was led by the Spirit into the wilderness to be tempted of the devil. After He passed the temptation, the Bible says, "the devil left Him, and behold, angels came and ministered to Him" (Matthew 4:11). Those angels were there to serve Him. The word that was translated *minister* from the Greek language (*diakoneó*) means "to serve, wait upon, to supply food or necessities of life."[8] Those angels were sent to bring refreshing to Him. I believe that the Lord sends angels with winds of refreshing into your life. They supply you with spiritual nourishment that infuses strength, force, might, and vigor from the Spirit of the Lord.

Speaking God's Word activates times of refreshing. When you speak the words of the Lord, angels move to accomplish what you've declared. "Bless the LORD, you His angels, who excel in strength, who do His word, heeding the voice of His word" (Psalm 103:20). Jesus spoke the Word in the face of temptation as the devil tried to deceive Him. The more He spoke what God said, the more angels gathered to minister to Him. Likewise, the more you speak what God has said, angels are gathering to minister strength to your spirit.

PRAYER

Father, I repent to You for my sin and all that I've allowed to hinder me from You and Your will for me. I ask for forgiveness. Convert, untwist, and realign my heart to be like You. Then let Your winds of refreshing flood my soul. Give me strength to stand against the schemes and plans of the enemy. Send angels—ministering spirits—to pour into me that I may stand in the days ahead. In Jesus' name, Amen.

A Quantum Leap

And it happened, when Elizabeth heard the greeting of Mary, that the babe leaped in her womb; and Elizabeth was filled with the Holy Spirit.

—Luke 1:41

I was ministering in a service a few years ago in the Washington, DC, area. As I began preaching a simple prophetic message on the shaking that God was beginning to bring in America and how the Church would rise up from that shaking with greater power, the Lord began to speak to me. He said to tell the people that they were about to experience a quantum leap in the Spirit. It was as if they would be propelled through time into acceleration. They would see Him speed up the fulfillment of prophetic words over their lives.

At the time, I didn't fully understand. I didn't know the exact definition of a quantum leap. All I knew is that as we worshiped and praised the Lord, many testimonies began to pour in about what God had done. God had begun to open major doors to nations for people there. What would have taken years was shortened by the hand of God. Websters Dictionary defines *quantum leap* as "an abrupt change, sudden increase, or dramatic advance."[9] This is what I believe is coming to the Body of Christ. We will experience an abrupt change for the better with transfers of sudden increase and a dramatic advancement. Get ready to see God propel you forward.

Quantum leap is a physics term. This definition gets a little more complex, but I want you to read it so that you might see the prophetic symbolism of it. God speaks through science. One of the descriptions of God is omniscient (omni—science). He is all knowing or all science (knowledge). Natural human science is trying to catch up with what God has done and what God has said. In physics, a quantum leap is a discontinuous transition between quantum states. What this means is that an electron in one energy level in an atom jumps instantly into another energy level, emitting or absorbing energy as it does so. There is no in-between state, and it doesn't take any time for the leap to occur.

The symbolism of this is God jumping you from one quantum level to another instantly, without any time in between. Only God could allow you to move into your next level with ease, grace, and an acceleration of time. Only God could cause you to traverse territory spiritually without the resistance, labor, or warfare. I believe that you are coming into a time where you will experience a quantum leap in your spirit.

How does this connect to Scripture in any way? Well, we can take a look at the story of Mary and Elizabeth:

> In those days Mary arose and went with haste into the hill country, to a town in Judah, and she entered the house of Zechariah and greeted Elizabeth. And when Elizabeth heard the greeting

of Mary, the baby leaped in her womb. And Elizabeth was filled
with the Holy Spirit, and she exclaimed with a loud cry, "Blessed
are you among women, and blessed is the fruit of your womb!
And why is this granted to me that the mother of my Lord
should come to me? For behold, when the sound of your greeting came to my ears, the baby in my womb leaped for joy. And
blessed is she who believed that there would be a fulfillment of
what was spoken to her from the Lord."

Luke 1:39–45 ESV

When Mary greeted Elizabeth, her baby leaped. Elizabeth
was pregnant with John the Baptist. There was a supernatural
occurrence in the greeting because their destinies were connected. John would prepare the way and Jesus would enter as
the Messiah. This spiritual motion that happened in her womb
was a divine impulse triggered by the Holy Spirit.

Then the Bible says that Elizabeth was filled with the Spirit.
This exchange was signified by a leap. The word *leap* is defined
as "to spring free from or to pass abruptly from one state to
another."[10] Prophetically, you are about to leap in the Spirit. You
will experience God transitioning you abruptly from one state
to another with great force. This will be by the power of God.
You will experience this as spiritual growth and development
in the giftings from the Lord that you carry.

You will experience a supernatural quantum leap in these
areas:

- Your faith—You will see an increase in your faith to believe God for the impossible. Don't be swayed by unbelief. As you yield to the Father and remain in His Word,
  you will leap forward in faith.

- Character development—You're going to experience phenomenal growth. After testing comes promotion. You will endure trials, but they will not consume you. You will build character and grow in the things of God.
- Your prayers—Just as Elizabeth was filled with the Holy Spirit, you, too, can have that experience. Being full of Holy Spirit power will give you persistence in prayer and fortification in your personal life. Intercession will intensify as you commune with the Father.
- Against resistance—You will see a quantum leap in your life that will cause you to stand against the resistance of the enemy. Whatever the devil tried against you will fail.

PRAYER

Father, let Your anointing of acceleration come upon me. I pray that I would quantum leap into the purpose and destiny that You have for me. Assist me to grow in You as never before. Help me to grow in my faith, character development, and prayer life. Fortify me to stand against the resistance of the enemy. Fill me with Your Holy Spirit even more. In Jesus' name, Amen.

WEEK 7

Strategic
Spiritual Warfare

The Weapon
of Strategic Rest

Speak to the Israelites and say to them: "When you enter the land I am going to give you, the land itself must observe a sabbath to the LORD. For six years sow your fields, and for six years prune your vineyards and gather their crops. But in the seventh year the land is to have a year of sabbath rest, a sabbath to the LORD. Do not sow your fields or prune your vineyards. Do not reap what grows of itself or harvest the grapes of your untended vines. The land is to have a year of rest."

—Leviticus 25:2–5 NIV

The Lord will never send you into a new season, territory, or appointment without giving you instructions on how you are to handle the new place and what to do when you get there. It's common for us to shout and fall out over a prophetic word declaring that we are about to occupy new land and territory, but the Lord says, *Let me show you how to govern yourself in this new place.* As you've come out of the last season, as difficult or successful as it was, it most likely did not come without some fight and warfare. And as God placed His anointing and seal upon you, you grew and expanded your territory. Where you were, where you have been over the past couple of years, is not the same as where you're headed. You are in a transition period right now, and although you thought the last season stretched you, you are about to expand once again.

In Leviticus 25, we find the people of Israel also about to enter a new land. Each line in this chapter is loaded with revelation, but I want to focus on the place where God says, "In the seventh year the land is to have a year of sabbath rest, a sabbath to the LORD" (verse 4) That's important. Hold on to that. He went on to tell them:

> "Do not sow your fields or prune your vineyards. Do not reap what grows of itself or harvest the grapes of your untended vines. The land is to have a year of rest. Whatever the land yields during the sabbath year will be food for you—for yourself, your male and female servants, and the hired worker and temporary resident who live among you, as well as for your livestock and the wild animals in your land. Whatever the land produces may be eaten."

Leviticus 25:4–7 NIV

In other words, He is declaring for them a year of rest. Rest is one of the most underrated weapons in a believer's spiritual warfare arsenal. Often in battle, the enemy uses the tactic of wearing down the resources and energy of its opponent, which causes them to lower their defenses and leave themselves open to attack. We see in Scripture where the enemy comes to a man or woman of God to make them vulnerable or weakened. We've seen examples of this in the lives of Adam and Eve (see Genesis 3:1–7), Samson (see Judges 16:15–21), and Christ (see Matthew 4:1–11). We know from our own experiences how when we are weary, we find it difficult to focus, and we are restless, impatient, indecisive, and prone to give into things we never would have had we been rested.

While rest is so much more than sleep, the Center for Disease Control and Prevention (CDC) compares sleep deprivation to alcohol intoxication.[1] When we are deprived of sleep and rest, we can exhibit the same kinds of mental and physical impairments as a drunk person! Rest is so important that our all-powerful God of the universe rested at the end of Creation week. And as God rested, He commands seasons of rest for His people.

What God has shown me is that we are coming into a period of rest. This rest functions as a reset enabling us to come back stronger, more fruitful, more discerning, and with a higher spiritual acuity and resistance to the enemy than ever before. This rest, or reset, is strategic and necessary for our performance in the next season. Let me show you what I mean.

When we look in Hebrew traditions, the Sabbath or seventh year is called *shmita*.[2] You may have heard it taught before, but I want to give you a different perspective. The *shmita* is in essence a reset for the land—not only for physical or natural land, but also for our spiritual land or territory. Whenever the Lord brings about a reset in your life, He is reordering it. He is changing everything in your world. The reality you know now is not the reality you will know in the coming days and months. The way that you see things now is not the way that you're going to see them in the days ahead. Everything is becoming new. As a result, you are about to see major doorways in the Spirit opened to you. Why? Because God is resetting your pathways. He's resetting your connections and covenants. He's resetting areas of your ministry, career, business, and family life.

In Hebrew, the word *shmita* literally means "release."[3] Following God's leading into this forty-day reset, look to Him to lead you into rest, reset, and a season of release. As you enter this season, you will see what has been held up and held back and the release of the promises of God for which you've been praying. Perhaps you have been praying and laboring for years for something you know God promised you. You've thought, *Lord, when is it going to happen? When am I going to see it come to pass? When are You going to do the thing that You said?* I hear the Lord saying that He has been waiting for this time and for this season. Your times have been pregnant with purpose, and you are about to give birth in the coming season.

You may have heard a message like this before, so I want to challenge you to get past the religious concepts, dogma, clichés you've heard. This is not that. I want you to really make this word personal. This isn't a cliché. It's not a sermon. This is a prophetic and apostolic word. The Lord said, *I'm about to bring release to My people. I'm going to open what has been closed. I'm going to open doors that have been shut. I'm going to open assignments that I promised to you, but you weren't ready for.* We are now coming into a moment of maturation in the Spirit where the Lord is saying, *Now, you are ready for that assignment. Now you are ready for that promise, and it's about to be released to you.* And it will not be about your labor, your warfare, or your works, for you will be at rest when it happens.

The Bible says that there should be a ceasing from plowing and working the land (see Leviticus 25). I want you to understand that what's about to come on you is a grace that you've not experienced before. The Lord is going to take all the labor you've done in your flesh and bring an end to it in the coming season. You will not do it in your flesh. You will not be able to do it by your mind or in your own strength. Instead, you will have to rest in God. You have been working so hard, pushing and trying to get to a place where you see victory and results. Get ready for those things to manifest.

Even as you rest on your land, the Lord said to me that you will also experience rest from all your enemies. You've been attacked by demonic spirits who were sent to cause you to abort what the Lord has given you, and you've fought well. But as you come into this next period, what you have been fighting is about to serve you. The thing that you've been warring against and the giants and the enemies you've been facing are about to be settled in your life. Your enemy is about to become your footstool. The one who has given you the greatest opposition is now going to be the one God uses to open a door of influence for you. Receive the rest of God in your life, and be ready to make a comeback no one saw coming.

PRAYER

Lord, I pray that You would bring me into a season of spiritual rest. Settle the striving, working, and warfare on my behalf. I rest in Your provision and peace as You reset my life. I look forward to being strengthened, revived, more discerning, and more fruitful in the coming seasons. In Jesus' name, Amen.

The Whole Armor of God

Finally, my brethren, be strong in the Lord and in the power of His might. Put on the whole armor of God, that you may be able to stand against the wiles of the devil. For we do not wrestle against flesh and blood, but against principalities, against powers, against the rulers of the darkness of this age, against spiritual hosts of wickedness in the heavenly places. Therefore take up the whole armor of God, that you may be able to withstand in the evil day, and having done all, to stand.

—Ephesians 6:10–13

God is jealous for His people—He is fiercely protective of us. He rises as Jehovah Gibbor, the God of war, when we are threatened. And while God will fight for us, He is also a wise Father who will teach us how to fight and win.

He teaches my hands to make war, so that my arms can bend a bow of bronze. You have also given me the shield of Your salvation; Your right hand has held me up, Your gentleness has made me great. You enlarged my path under me, so my feet did not slip. I have pursued my enemies and overtaken them; neither did I turn back again till they were destroyed.

Psalm 18:34–37

In Psalm 144:1, we read, "Blessed be the LORD my Rock, who trains my hands for war, and my fingers for battle." Now, if you've not always been saved, sanctified, and filled with the Holy Ghost, and any talk about a fight gets you excited, let me clarify the kind of fighting God is training us for. From our key verse for today, we learn that "we do not wrestle against flesh and blood, but against principalities, against powers, against the rulers of the darkness of this age, against spiritual hosts of wickedness in the heavenly places" (verse 12).

This is a spiritual battle, which also means you'll have to put those boxing gloves away, because the weapons God wants us to arm ourselves with are not physical, human, or fleshly weapons. "For the weapons of our warfare are not carnal but mighty in God for pulling down strongholds" (2 Corinthians 10:4).

The evil day for which God is preparing us to withstand is upon us. We are living in a time of great darkness, and even though God has already secured the victory, there are still battles we must fight. God is not only teaching us to fight these battles, but He's also given us both an armor to protect ourselves and a strategy to use what He's given to take down enemy strongholds.

In our key verse, we read that God is instructing us to "put on the whole armor of God, that you may be able to stand against the wiles of the devil." I'm going to break down the armor and what each piece is. But first, let's deal with what we're up against. Let's look at this word *wiles*.

Wiles are "stratagems meant to fool, trap, or entice."[4] Seducing spirits fight with devious stratagems. A stratagem is a cunning plan or scheme. Seducing spirits will plan out and manipulate events and situations in order to get a desired reaction out of their target. This is done to gain access to his or her soul. They may influence someone close to their target to speak certain words or take actions that, depending on the targeted person's response, can give seducing spirits access to his or her soul. This is why it is important that you guard what you say and do in response to things that happen in your life. Make sure that you are in line with the Word of God so that you do not open a door to the enemy.

The only way to firmly stand up against the wiles of the devil is to have on the whole armor of God, which protects you entirely. Here's what the Bible outlines as the armor of God:

> Take up the whole armor of God, that you may be able to withstand in the evil day, and having done all, to stand. Stand therefore, having girded your waist with truth, having put on the breastplate of righteousness, and having shod your feet with the preparation of the gospel of peace; above all, taking the shield of faith with which you will be able to quench all the fiery darts of the wicked one. And take the helmet of salvation, and the sword of the Spirit, which is the word of God; praying always with all prayer and supplication in the Spirit.

Ephesians 6:13–18

Let's look at each piece of armor and the work it does to secure you against enemy attacks.

1. The Belt of Truth

In order to understand the function of this piece of armor and what it means to have "your loins girt about with truth" (verse 14 KJV), you need to get a clear understanding of Hebrew clothing worn during ancient times. A tunic was the basic, essential garment worn by Jews—both men and women. The men's tunic was shorter; it was about knee length and more colorful than the women's version of it. The women's tunic was most often an ankle length, full robe. They would wear an undergarment known as a loincloth, girdle, or small waist covering. This would be worn under the regular garments.

In most cases, the girdle was made of cloth or leather and was used like a belt to hold a person's tunic to his or her waist. The girdle was also used to hold weapons, tools, and money.

When men would run, work, or fight, they would tuck the hem of the tunic inside the girdle to gain more movement. This was known as "girding your loins." The phrase became symbolic for preparedness. Paul uses this phrase in our key passage, as Peter used it in 1 Peter 1:13, as a command to have a sober mind and to be alert and ready. Girding your loins with truth means making yourself spiritually ready and prepared by walking in the Spirit of truth.[5]

2. The Breastplate of Righteousness

The breastplate of righteousness is a covering to guard one of the most vital organs in the body—the heart. The heart represents the soul and essence of a person. "Keep your heart with all diligence, for out of it spring the issues of life" (Proverbs

4:23). Everything flows from the heart. It is the enemy's job to try to compromise your heart to detour you from the path of righteousness. We must put on the spiritual breastplate of righteousness as a protective measure against enemies of our soul and emotions. The heart can be full of compassion but also dangerously blind when emotionally compromised.

3. The Shoes of the Gospel of Peace

Feet are symbolic of the path or direction in which you will go. We must all make sure that we are walking in the pathway of the Gospel of Jesus Christ. The early Church in the book of Acts was not originally called Christians. Believers were known as those who walk in the way. The way of the Lord is perfect (see Psalm 18:30). The way of the Lord is secure (see Proverbs 14:26). The way of the Lord brings peace; however, the path to peace may at times be contentious and may attract attacks since we have an enemy who works contrary to our peace.

To *shod* one's feet means "to bind under one's feet, i.e., to put on shoes or sandals."[6] Shoes or sandals provide covering and protection for our feet; therefore, to shod your feet with the preparation of the Gospel of peace means doing what's necessary to bind your direction to the Word and keep your steps in the way of righteousness.

4. The Shield of Faith

Faith is the most vital tool that we have as believers. The devil's age-old tactic has been to launch arrows of doubt, fear, and unbelief at our mind to influence how we think. He ultimately hopes to corrupt our behavior and make us walk away from God. Consistently strengthen your faith by abiding in the Word of God.

5. Helmet of Salvation

A helmet is protective equipment designed to guard the head of someone in combat or sport. When someone experiences trauma, whether or not they are wearing a helmet can be the difference between a brain injury or a small headache. The brain is the central processing unit of the body and the natural representation of the mind. Paul tells us that the mind must be renewed (see Romans 12:2). The mind must be saved in order to see God. Accepting Christ as your personal Savior is the first step in renewing your mind. Reading, studying, and hiding the Word of the Lord in your heart is how you guard and cover your mind. That is how you put on the helmet of salvation.

6. The Sword of the Spirit

The sword of the Spirit is the Word of God. A sword cuts. As it is in the natural, so it is in the spiritual realm. The Word of God has the power to cut away anything in the heart, mind, spirit, or soul that could separate us from God. When we read and apply His Word, impurities, faulty beliefs, and faithlessness are uprooted. In addition, I believe that praying the Word of God is using the sword of the Spirit to annihilate diabolical plans.

Every one of these pieces of armor must be put on, which is a deliberate action and is meant "in the sense of sinking into a garment."[7] We must take them up and clothe ourselves in them all. If we are missing even one piece, we are left open to attack.

PRAYER

Lord, I pray that You would increase my awareness of the spiritual battle raging around me and that I would know that You are my refuge and my hedge against the enemy. Empower me to put on the spiritual armor that You've given me and protect me from all evil. Fight against the demonic weapons that war against my soul. In Jesus' name, Amen.

Sweatless Victory

The LORD will fight for you, and you shall hold your peace.

—Exodus 14:14

Even as there are demonic agendas and darkness rising within the earth with panic and anxiety being common responses, we must learn how to stand in the peace of God and in faith knowing God has already covered us. He has already taken care of every need. We don't have to panic. We don't have to be anxious. We don't have to live in fear, worry, and doubt. God has got this. Some things are not your battle. They are not your fight. The Lord has already fought for you in the challenge you are facing, and you will experience what I call a sweatless victory. Make this your declaration as you reset and transition. Begin to prepare today for the new thing God has lined up for you.

The Lord Will Fight for You

There is an aspect of the character of God that I believe we are going to see as never before. We've seen Him as love. We have seen Him as goodness, mercy, and grace. And all of those things are very true when it comes to who God is. But the God we are about to see is Jehovah Gibbor, the God of war. God is about to stand up and fight for His people.

God led me into a vision where I saw attacks coming upon the people of God. But, then I saw the Lord stand up in a war-like position. I saw that He sent angels to come to our rescue. The angels of the Lord were being sent out on assignment to bring the strength, healing, and resources we need for this time. The Lord said to me that help is coming—the help of God is on the way. When it comes, you may feel it as if the wind of God is blowing on you, giving you the push that you need. Or you may feel an influx of strength come up in your spirit and in your body. Whatever you've been going through, whatever you need to win the battle, the Lord says, *I'm sending help*.

The angels of God are on assignment now, and they are going to bring a ceasefire to the warfare you've been dealing with. You may be dealing with mental warfare—anxiety, depression, exhaustion, or discouragement. Whatever you've been facing, the Lord says, *Get ready for a ceasefire in the spirit*.

Nahum says, "God is jealous, and the Lord avenges" (Nahum 1:2). The definition of this word *jealous* is one of the perspectives of God that we don't hear mentioned often, and many people misinterpret its use in this verse. They think of it being used in the same way we use *jealous* in our current vernacular. Some may think, "Well, how is the Lord jealous?" What it really says here is that God is jealous *for us*. Whatever the Lord creates—and we are His creation—He is protective of. This means that He loves you so much that He is going to defend you.

So, whatever enemy has been opposing you, whatever demonic force has been coming against you, whatever attacks are occurring against your mind—whether you're dealing with oppression, thoughts of suicide, or other mental battles—I want you to know that God loves you so much that He says, *I'm violent toward the enemy that's coming against you right now. I will defend you. I will stand up for you. You only need to be still.*

As you remain still and let the Lord fight for you, peace will come upon you out of nowhere. In the midst of your chaos, right in the place where anxiety and panic try to take up residence, the peace of the Lord is coming. When that peace comes, you will know it is the Holy Spirit invading your space. You will know the presence of the Lord is there in that very place.

If God Isn't Worried, Neither Should You Be

I've learned that if God isn't worried about it, I shouldn't be either. Think about the disciples who went out to sea with Jesus as a violent storm erupted and the winds and waves beat against the sides of their boat (see Luke 8:22–25). The disciples began to panic because they thought that the boat was going to turn over and that they were going to drown.

Where was Jesus in all this? He was asleep in the boat. You know this story. They were panicking. "Master, do you care that we are perishing?" They were so worked up and afraid that they began to question His care even though they had seen Him supply their needs and provide for them. He had walked with them and taught them. He had done life with them. And, yet, in so many words, they questioned whether or not He cared about them. "Lord, do You even care that we are in the middle of this storm and are about to drown?"

If we are real with ourselves, we can admit that it is one of the worst feelings to have when it seems as though our life is falling apart. We interpret God's silence as His lack of care for us. But let me give you two new perspectives you can build on.

1. You're in transition. When you are in a storm and God is silent—you're not getting any word, there is no breakthrough, there is no kind of confirmation from the Lord, you enter into prayer and you're not hearing much—this silence may indicate that you are in transition. The page is turning, you are going from one side to the other (as the disciples were), and a new chapter is about to begin. Let me assure you: God may be silent, but He is there in the boat with you.

2. He has already taken care of the situation. Understand that when God is silent, He is not panicked or concerned. And if He's not concerned, then He's already taken care of the situation you're in. Learn to trust the Holy Spirit as He's leading you through life. When you are going through your hard trial and you feel as though God is absent and He's not speaking, know that He is there. If He's not talking to you about it, then He has already taken care of it. All you need to do is relax. No amount of effort you put toward it is going to change that storm. It's going to take the One who created the weather—the winds and the waves of the sea—to rise up and speak to His creation and command it to be calm. Jesus has already spoken to your storm.

We are coming into a time where it will not be by our might, our power, or the sweat of our brow but by the Spirit of the Lord that our battles are fought and won. Learn to rest in and receive His sweatless victory.

PRAYER

Father, I receive You as Jehovah Gibbor. I will stand still and see Your salvation. Release angels on my behalf. Bring help where I've needed it. If there's been any time that I have tried to step in and do things my own way and in my own strength, I repent and surrender all to You. I welcome Your peace and will rest in the sweatless victories You win for me. In Jesus' name, Amen.

Dismantling Fear

Have I not commanded you? Be strong and of good courage;
do not be afraid, nor be dismayed, for the LORD your God is
with you wherever you go.

—Joshua 1:9

With so much negativity happening around us in the world—the crises, the disunity, the anger, the violence, the isolation, and the grief—it can be devastating. The things we're seeing and experiencing can cause fear and even a spirit of fear—and there is a difference between the two. The Bible tells us that God has not given us the spirit of fear, but He's given us power, love, and a sound mind (see 2 Timothy 1:7). Greater than natural human fear, a spirit of fear comes with torment. A spirit of fear is not natural. It's very different from the fear you may feel when you see a snake. Fear in this case is a signal to let you know there's danger.

A spirit of fear, on the other hand, is oppressive and often comes with panic and anxiety. A spirit of fear comes with a demonic agenda to pull you out of faith and bring you into a place of doubt. In Joshua 1, we come across Joshua at a place in his life where, I can imagine, he was afraid and didn't know exactly what to do. He was in the midst of a major transition where he was taking on a daunting leadership role. While he had been prepared for it, he was caught off guard. Moses was dead, and Joshua had to lead the millions of people into the land of promise.

In verse 9, the Lord says, "Have I not commanded you? Be strong and courageous." What He's putting to Joshua, and to us, in this passage is not a suggestion. It's not just something nice to consider. "Well, maybe you can, you know, be strong." No, this is a command from the Lord. We are in some of the most unusual times during which it will take us putting on the strength of God to deal with many of the things that are happening now and in the days to come with courage.

When you see challenges up ahead in the world, you must be strong. When you find yourself in difficult or challenging situations, gaining the victory and maintaining your peace will require supernatural strength. This is not strength you can pull from your own flesh. It's not a strength that you can pull from a self-help book or a motivational speech. I'm talking about the strength of God that comes only by the empowerment of the Spirit of God. It is the Holy Ghost who empowers us to complete our assignments. It is the Holy Spirit who empowers us to accomplish things in the earth.

God wouldn't tell Joshua to be strong if he was not going to need that strength. If God gives you the command to be strong, understand that you are going to need it. As I share this with you, I'm reminded of a passage in Luke 21. It's where Jesus was talking about the tumultuous times that would come at the end of an age in which they were living, which is very much like the age in which we are living. We also have come to the end of an era and are transitioning to a new place in time.

When I read this passage, I'm always very pensive because it makes me wonder how the enemy could use this weapon of fear to attack believers. Let's look at verse 26. "Men's hearts failing them from fear and the expectation of those things which are coming on the earth, for the powers of the heavens will be shaken." Jesus is letting the people know that there will be a time when there will be so much calamity, disaster, and tragedy that men's hearts will begin to fail them due to fear.

This verse tells us just how powerful fear can be if we allow it to move in. This kind of fear has a deadly impact on our physical bodies. Heart failure is the spirit of fear. So, my encouragement to you today is to bind the spirit of fear in Jesus' name. This is the first task on the list for dismantling fear. No matter what you see going on around you and no matter what you see in the coming months, you must not panic. Why? Because you have access to the peace of God that surpasses all understanding.

Even in the midst of chaos and storms, you can be rooted and grounded in the Lord. When you face situations where you're wondering how you are going to come out on the other side, God is saying, *I'm right here with you. My peace I give to you; not as the world gives do I give to you. Let not your heart be troubled, neither let it be afraid for I will never leave you or forsake you* (see John 14:27; Deuteronomy 31:6). In the midst of everything going on, know that God is with you. Even now, declare this and speak this word from your mouth.

God is with you everywhere you go. He's there in every situation. Even when He's silent, even when you've been praying and you don't hear Him speaking to you, He is right there with you, leading you, guiding you, protecting you, and comforting you. So be strong, and don't panic.

As we look back at our key verse for today, Joshua 1:9, let's take a deeper dive into this word *strong*. The Hebrew language is powerful. As we look at the original text, we come across several definitions. The first one I'd like to focus on is "to fasten upon," or "attach to."[8] When God commands Joshua to be strong, in essence, He's saying, *You need to grab onto My Word, fasten yourself to My Word, and bind yourself to My Word. You need to bind My Word to your heart.* This is another important strategy in dismantling fear.

Obeying God's command to be strong is not anything you can do in the natural. You cannot pull from your own natural strength to be strong the way God means it. The fullness of this ability comes only when you draw from His Word. And this is why God says to Joshua that he must meditate on His Word both day and night. He said, "This Book of the Law shall not depart from your mouth, but you shall meditate in it day and night" (Joshua 1:8).

What are you fastened to? What are you holding on to? What word are you holding on to? Whose voice is the most powerful voice in your life? Because I guarantee you that the voice that you listen to the most is going to dictate your future. If you are holding onto the voice of fear, or a friend, or family member, it is not going to get you very far. You must gravitate to the Word of God and listen to the voice of God through His written Word.

The Bible is the most important book you'll ever read. When we've been in church for many years, we can sometimes read the Word and feel as if we've already read a certain passage before. We've heard it preached before, and so we want to hear something new. It's not always about this quest to find a new word. Sometimes we need to go back, get the same word we heard before, meditate on it, and rehearse that word in our spirit until it becomes alive in us. We must be careful not to fall into a trap of the enemy that causes us to always chase something new. Sometimes what we need is what we have already been taught. When we rehearse God's Word, it builds our faith and strengthens our hearts so that we can face down fear and move forward in courage and faith (see Romans 10:17).

PRAYER

Lord, I pray that You would strengthen my heart for the days ahead. Strengthen my spirit for the things that are coming, for the challenges I'm going to face, and the things I'm going to see play out in my world. Set my eyes on You. Put my focus on You. Let me not waver or doubt even when I see troubling things occur.

As I fasten myself to Your Word, I pray that You would raise the level of my faith. Cause my faith to rise. I bind the spirit of fear and doubt in Jesus' name. I take authority over every mind-binding spirit that comes to oppress me and cause me to waver from Your Word.

I will not waver in what You've told me—I will remember Your words. I will stand strong in courage and faith. I am established in Your Word. Father, thank You for supernatural strength. Increase it in me today. In Jesus' name, Amen.

Fasting and Prayer

This kind does not go out except by prayer and fasting.

—Matthew 17:21

At least once a year, and oftentimes more, the Lord puts it on my spirit to lead my church and those connected to our ministry in a fast. Many times, He leads us to fast as one month, year, or season ends and a new one is about to begin. It's important for those of us who are prophetic—and really every believer—to seek the heart of God during transitional times. We need to align ourselves to understand where we've been out of joint, and then, going forward, we need to come into agreement with the will of the Father.

Fasting is not always connected with driving a demon out of someone or some region. Sometimes fasting is a way for us to stay clean and clear of demonic influences and works of the flesh that could hinder us from operating in the full power of God's anointing on our lives. As we go about our assignments, we don't want to end up like the sons of Sceva who were beaten and run out of a house by a demonized man they thought they could deliver (see Acts 19:11–20). The Bible says, "Then the man in whom the evil spirit was leaped on them, overpowered them, and prevailed against them, so that they fled out of that house naked and wounded" (verse 16). We don't want the devil running us out of our assignments naked and wounded, so we must fast to allow our flesh to be subdued, submitted, and humbled before God.

The psalmist says that he humbled his soul with fasting (see Psalm 69:10). Humility is the key to receiving God's grace. "But He gives more grace. Therefore He says: 'God resists the proud, but gives grace to the humble.' Therefore submit to God. Resist the devil and he will flee from you" (James 4:6–7). We need God's grace, as it is His supernatural empowerment to live for Him and to serve Him as He commands. Fasting builds your resistance against the devil.

As much as we may be ready to use fasting in our strategy for casting out demons and operating effectively in spiritual warfare, fasting with prayer should also be part of the consecration process as we prepare to do greater things for the Kingdom of God. Fasting brings humility, and that helps us to be open to assessing what is not right within us. We can open ourselves to seek the face of God to ask, *Father, is there something in me that is not right? Is there pride in me that You see? Is there something in me that is not pleasing to You?*

These times of consecration are when we begin to ask the Lord to take out anything in us that is not like Him. We don't want to go into a new year, a new month, or a new chapter of our lives or ministry carrying the same old baggage. I know it's more popular these days for people to place the emphasis on other people in their lives who may not be right for them or who may be holding them back, but the emphasis should be on us. Our prayer needs to be, *What is in me, Father, that is not like You? Whatever You find, I humble myself so that You can take those things out of me.*

Again, before we can deal with the ungodly stuff around us, we need to ask God to clean up what's in us. I'm not talking about being super religious or super spiritual; however, internal deliverance and healing is a part of the journey of consecration. It's a part of the Lord pulling us in so that He can recalibrate, refresh, and refuel us for the journey ahead. If we don't come into the presence of the Lord and really align with His heart, we could miss out on what the Lord is about to do in the next move. So, as you transition from the old to the new, you may find the Holy Spirit leading you into times of prayer and fasting.

The Lord often gives us direction on how we are to fast. In the Bible, fasting is often connected with a restriction of food. That could be whole meals and for days at a time as it was with Moses in Exodus 34:8, Esther in Esther 4:16, and Christ in Matthew 4:2, or going without certain kinds of food as Daniel and his friends did in Daniel 1:11–16, and Daniel again on his own in Daniel 10:2–3. To combat our world with all its pleasures and distractions, God may lead us into different kinds of fasts. The key is to listen for His leading and follow it. If you are part of a local body, being in agreement with how your church community is praying and fasting is another way to add power to your times of consecration.

Ready for War

Once we've dealt with the stuff in us that could hinder our ability to hear from God and be effective in carrying out His will, we can expect to have the authority and power we need to effect change and push back darkness in the earth. In this effort, we must understand that prayer is our number one goal and force. Then we must understand that there are times we must couple prayer and intercession with fasting to see a specific kind of mountain or demonic power move. And even still, there are times after we have prayed and fasted that we still don't see things in the natural line up with what God has said, so we must begin again and continue in those things. In other words, do them again. Repeat what you have already done until you see victory, until you see the Lord move.

As I've prophesied many times on my Monday social media broadcasts, dark and evil times are upon us. While God does defend and shield His people from much of it, we still have a role to play in expanding the Kingdom and bringing heaven to earth despite the growing darkness. The Lord told me that through our intercession, we will see a lessening of these things. We will see our families and communities protected if we begin to raise the hedge. The word *hedge* is used in the King James Version and older translations of Ezekiel 22:30. "I sought for a man among them, that should make up the hedge, and stand in the gap." The word hedge is synonymous with wall, fence, or protective barrier. Our prayer, confessing God's Word, and living life in alignment with Him is a protective barrier against the enemy.

The word of the Lord to you for your church or group of intercessors is this: Raise the hedge. Raise the hedge in prayer, fasting, and intercession over your church, family, community, city, and state. Your prayer can shut down demonic attacks that the enemy is forming against you. The Bible says that there are some forces that do not move "except by prayer and fasting"

(Matthew 17:21). Prayer is the most powerful tool we have. We can never underestimate the power and the ability that we have in and through prayer. So, I'm encouraging you. Pray without ceasing. Your prayer is effective against the kingdom of darkness, because when we pray, the Lord moves. Prayer is the vehicle by which God moves in the earth.

God has called you and handpicked you for this time. Never underestimate the power of your prayer and your times of fasting. Never think that your prayer is not enough or that it won't make a difference. Your prayer matters, and it is needed.

PRAYER

Father, I thank You for alerting me to the times when Your Spirit is calling me into a time of prayer and fasting, a time of consecration. Thank You for keeping me aware of the enemy's schemes and giving me effective strategies to resist him. As I continue to navigate this time of recalibration and reset, please show me anything that is not in line with Your will. Set me straight. Set me on the right path. Strengthen me for the battles ahead. I humble myself under Your mighty hand, and I look forward to the coming victories. In Jesus' name, Amen.

WEEK 8

Revolutionize Your Life

Reset Your Words– Confessions

Set a guard, O LORD, over my mouth; keep watch over the door of my lips.

—Psalm 141:3

Every time the Lord brings the Body of Christ into a new era, He gives us a new spiritual vernacular or language to usher in that time. So, if you are still holding on to the old thing from 25 or 30 years ago, I'm telling you that God is releasing a new word and a new refreshing for this season. The word that accompanied the world you were born into will not work in the same world/age you live in now. Don't be left behind. Update your language.

We must become aware, knowledgeable, and in tune with the Spirit so that we know how to navigate the times we're in. We don't want to be left behind. Studies on the Church have found that it is about twenty years behind the world. What this means is that when it comes to our presentation, technology, leadership methodologies, and the way we carry out tasks, we are behind the world. And it's difficult for the Church as an institution to catch up because change is happening so rapidly.

If you have a smart phone, then you know how it is. We get updates all the time. Changes are continually being made. We're constantly getting a new alert to let us know that one of the apps we have needs to be updated. As it is in the natural, so it is in the spirit. There are things happening in the spirit world all around us, and many times the people of God are not in tune with or aware of what God is doing. This is why both the prophetic and apostolic dimensions are important to the Church. They give us a clear path concerning what's happening right now, and they give us a clear picture of what God is doing in the earth.

One of the things God has been showing me is that we need to reset our words. How we speak to ourselves and others about what's happening in our lives or the world around us matters. Having our words be in line with God's Word influences our ability to see the word of the Lord come to pass. So, we must align our speech with the new place God is taking us. Let's look at how the precedent for this is established in the Bible.

In Acts 2, the Bible tells us about the 120 believers praying and waiting for the coming of the Holy Spirit in the Upper Room. Christ had instructed them to wait before He ascended to heaven. Just as Jesus promised, there was an outpouring from the Spirit of God, and He sat on them like cloven tongues of fire. You know this story, but there are a few things I want to point out.

First, there was the sound of a mighty rushing wind. God came with the sound before He manifested Himself. What we can learn from this is that the Lord will always release a sound before He manifests. This is why whenever the seasons begin to change, you need to tune your ears into the prophetic voices that God has assigned to your life and to the Body of Christ, because those who can truly hear from God will begin to pick up the sound of heaven and echo what the Lord is saying.

Then after the sound of the mighty rushing wind, God gave them a special language, which is known as *glossolalia*. This word carries two meanings. The first is that you are supernaturally given the ability to speak a language you did not speak before. Others who speak that language are able to understand, even while you don't understand what is being said. The second meaning refers to the language we pray in, which is praying in the Spirit in a heavenly language. When God released this language, He released it to accompany a new move of the Spirit. The precedent of God giving us new words when He begins to move was set in Acts 2. He does this to explain what's about to happen. So, if you have your ear to the heartbeat of God, He'll begin to speak new words that will usher you into His next move.

A Season to Speak Life

In the Old Testament, God gave the people of Israel a choice. After He had given them instructions on how to prosper by following His ways, as well as telling them what could happen if they didn't, He said, "I call heaven and earth as witnesses today against you, that I have set before you life and death, blessing and cursing; therefore choose life, that both you and your descendants may live" (Deuteronomy 30:19). In this new era, our words must match the choices we've made to follow God and align with His plans for our lives.

The enemy of our soul has released a spirit of death and destruction in our communities. We must not come into agreement with him by the words we speak. Speaking life in this new day is more important than ever before. We must let God purify our tongues with coals from His altar (see Isaiah 6:6–7). We cannot let any vain speech or careless words slip from our lips. Words have power, and as seeds are sown, every word has fruit. We will reap a harvest from the words we speak (see Matthew 12:36).

The Lord has shown me that we're going to see an epic battle between death and life. In this battle, He has anointed us to speak life. So, when the enemy is saying that it's a season of death, we can stand up and say, "No. The Lord says this is our season to live."

When we speak life, we speak the language of heaven, of peace, joy, and righteousness in the Holy Spirit. When we speak life, we elevate Jesus, and we take the power away from those dark entities. When we speak life, we begin to put the focus back on the main thing. Because when you come in agreement with God to speak life and carry His Word in your mouth, you will reap a harvest as you have never seen before.

Speak life to yourself—about your family, business, finances, and ministry—and long-awaited promises will come to pass. Speak life, and you will find yourself in a harvest season in which the promises God gave you twenty years ago will begin to manifest. You'll begin to see prophetic words that were spoken over your life five years ago begin to manifest. Those words you received in prayer that caused you to write in your journal, "God, this sounds too crazy for me to even imagine that this could come to pass," will be fulfilled. You will get to watch God begin to manifest it. When God resets your words, your confession, you will see a harvest of those words. You will see the manifestation of the promises of God over your life.

PRAYER

Father, I pray that as I learn the new language for this season, I will keep my ear pressed to Your lips. I will speak only as You direct. When the enemy speaks death, I will speak life. I will not allow my words to tear down what God is trying to build in my life. So, with the psalmist I pray, "Set a guard, over my mouth; keep watch over the door of my lips." In Jesus' name, Amen.

Reset Your Mind–
Thinking Differently

As [a man] thinks in his heart, so is he.
—Proverbs 23:7

We can ask God to increase us a thousand times more than we already are (see Deuteronomy 1:11). I believe that we are in a time when the increase of God is upon us. His increase is not always manifested in money or material possessions. The increase I see coming is an increase to your soul. "Beloved, I pray that you may prosper in all things and be in health, just as your soul prospers" (3 John 1:2). God will only prosper you to the level of your soul's prosperity.

Your soul is your innermost being made up of your mind, will, and emotions. So, if God is going to increase you at the soul level, this means that your character must come in alignment with God. This means that your soul must be in order. This means that you are operating from a renewed mind. This means that your emotions are in check, and you aren't living with rejection, bitterness, anger, unforgiveness, divisiveness, or lust of the flesh, eyes, and pride. This means that you must lay aside sins, weights, and everything that is not pleasing to the Lord.

In order for your soul to be ready for God's increase, you must start with a renewed mind. The Bible tells us that we are transformed by the renewing of our mind (see Romans 12:2). Our mind and the way we think dictates who we are, as Proverbs 23:7—our verse for today—states. And who we are influences the life we live and the choices we make. What's interesting about this verse is that it doesn't say, "As a man thinks in his mind, so is he." It says as a man thinks in his heart. Can a heart think? Yes, it can, and here's proof.

According to the original Hebrew, the word used for *heart*, *nepeš*, refers to the "soul, self, mind, desire, emotion, and the inner being of man."[1] Going further, we find that the word *heart* also refers to "seat of appetites" and "seat of emotions and passions."[2] So we can see that, in essence, the words *soul*, *heart*, and *mind* can be used interchangeably when referring to the place within us from which our thoughts derive.

We often say that people follow their hearts or that they are led by their emotions—and sometimes we don't mean this as a compliment. We tend to think of following your heart or being led by your emotions as negative or impractical. But if we accept what the Word is showing us, we see that we are governed by our hearts. What we should want to see, however, is that as we are led by what we think or feel, those thoughts and feelings are submitted to the will of God. As we think, we are to think His thoughts. As we desire things in life and aspire to achieve higher levels in our personal, professional, or spiritual lives, we allow Him to shape those desires and aspirations so that they align with His plans for us. As we are moved in our emotions, we are calibrating them to the truth of His Word. This is why we must pursue God's transformational process—so that He can renew or reset our mind and bring our will into submission to His will.

One of the most effective ways to reset your mind is to allow the Word of God, the Bible, to take root in your heart. Yes, this means you must center your mental reset around regular Bible study and Bible reading. So many in the Church today are biblically illiterate. They can come to church each week, shout, speak in tongues, and put on a good Christian face, but they are beat up in their mind and emotions throughout the week. We can live differently. It does not have to be this way for us. We have a guide on how to live a free and blessed life.

Psalm 119:105 says that God's Word is a lamp to our feet and light to our path. His Word is a guiding light for our lives. If we are wondering what is right or wrong, we can turn to His Word for revelation. When Joshua was getting ready to lead the people of Israel after Moses had died, I can imagine how he may have been overcome with fearful and self-defeating thoughts. God knew the mental attack he would face, so He commanded Joshua to meditate on His Word day and night (see Joshua 1:8). Paul tells us exactly of what our thoughts should be comprised:

> Whatever things are true, whatever things are noble, whatever things are just, whatever things are pure, whatever things are lovely, whatever things are of good report, if there is any virtue and if there is anything praiseworthy—meditate [or think] on these things.
>
> Philippians 4:8

The hard part in this mind-renewal process is making the choice to *do* what the Word says: to practice and become skilled in being able to think in line with God through the Spirit. But the Bible says we deceive ourselves if we think we can be hearers of the Word only and not doers also (see James 1:22). If we want to be transformed, we must do what God is saying to us about how to have a mind stayed on Him. So, you will have to choose to fill your mind daily, and sometimes moment by moment, with the truth of God's Word. You will have to choose to take your thoughts captive (see 2 Corinthians 10:5) and not allow negative, evil, or unsubmitted thoughts to run freely in your mind.

You will have to choose to rejoice always and remain thankful (see Philippians 4:4). Give God praise even when it seems as if all hell is breaking loose and you're tempted to fear, worry, or complain. God inhabits your praise (see Psalm 22:3). Let Him dwell in your worship and thanksgiving. Where He is, there is fullness of joy and peace that passes all understanding.

Worship keeps God as our main focus. It keeps our eyes on Him. You can't worship and worry at the same time. You can't worship and compare your life to someone else's. You can't worship and gossip. Bitter and sweet cannot come from the same spring (see James 3:10–12). Thank God for the work He is doing in your life, for the breakthroughs you have seen in the past, for the victories He's won on your behalf, and for the healing, the miracles, and the provision you've experienced. Make sure you stay in remembrance of the goodness of God. The enemy will try to throw stumbling blocks and distractions into your journey toward renewal, but when you can think of the goodness of God and all He's done for you, your soul will be renewed and refreshed.

Keep your expectations high. Believe for the best outcomes. Cast down imaginations and thoughts that don't line up with what God has shown you. Don't be afraid to have hope even in the darkest times. God will not fail you.

As you begin to think differently, your soul will increase in prosperity. You may have been in a spiritually dry place, but as your mind is set on things above, you should get ready for rivers to begin to flow in the middle of your desert place. You are coming to a fruitful and flourishing place where you will not want for anything. God is about to prosper you even as your renewed and reset soul prospers.

PRAYER

Lord, I thank You for the challenge of this word today. I need a mind reset. I need to think on new levels in preparation for the new place to which You are bringing me. Even as I welcome the transition into a new day and chapter in my life, I commit to being transformed by the renewing of my mind and heart. Shape my innermost being and make it like You. I take responsibility for choosing to follow You on this journey, for feeding my mind with the truth of Your Word, and for meditating on it day and night. I thank You in advance for increasing my soul's prosperity. In Jesus' name, Amen.

Reset Your Relationships

Walk with the wise and become wise, for a companion of fools suffers harm.

—Proverbs 13:20 NIV

At the end of every year, people begin to post on social media about who they are cutting off and leaving so that they can move into the new year free and unhindered. While this practice has some merit, we need to go deeper than that. Who you have in your life reflects more about you than it does about them, so it may not be as simple as cutting them off. God created us for connection and relationship with other humans, but godly wisdom must be applied in discerning how they are to be connected to us and what role they should serve in helping us live out God's plan for our lives.

Throughout Jesus' ministry, He maintained relationships with all kinds of people. There were the multitudes He had compassion for and healed (see Matthew 9:36, 15:32), the Pharisees—His critics—whom He held at arm's length (see Matthew 23), the 72 He trained and sent out to minister on His behalf (see

Luke 10:1–23), the women who prayed for Him, provided care and hospitality, financially supported His ministry, and served alongside Him (see Matthew 28:1–10; Mark 16; Luke 1, 2, 8:1–3, 10:38–42, 24:1–12; John 11:1–44), the twelve disciples He traveled and did life with and the inner circle (see Matthew 10:2–4; Mark 3:14–19; Luke 6:13–16), the core group of three—Peter, James, and John—with whom He prayed and shared His most vulnerable moments (see Matthew 17:1, 26:36–46; Mark 14:32–42).

Using Jesus as a model, can you identify all the relationships you hold and what category into which each person falls? You may not be able to answer this right now, but this should be a relationship inventory exercise you take on with patience and prayer during this reset season. There could be people you need to cut out of your life, but there could also be some Spirit-led reassigning you may need to do.

You are not the same person you were yesterday when certain people came into your life. You didn't know what you know now. God hadn't done as much work in your life as He has done now. There has been revelation, healing, and pruning that has taken place. The work that He's begun in you should cause you to see people differently, which means it may be time to allow God to lead you through a relationship reset.

With a reset like this, you will need to be willing to let go of the old. There may be some old connections the Lord will have you release. There are old circles that are no longer serving the purpose for which you initially joined them. There may be some people you let go of in the past because of pride or offense with whom you now need to forgive and reconcile. It's time to release the old to get the new. In order for you to move into new things, new places, new people, new connections, and new areas, you must be willing to allow the old to be broken down and reset. The Bible says that we shouldn't put new wine into old wine skin (see Luke 5:37).

You can't put the new outpouring of God into an old infrastructure because it cannot handle it. It doesn't have the capacity. As you're turning the page and entering a new chapter of life, God will send you new relationships. You can't put them into the same old crowd, the same old system, and the same old territory. To be open to this full reset, you must be willing to take inventory of the relationships you kept to see what new thing God wants to release over your networks and associations.

The newness of God is upon you. You are in a new day. You are even going to look different when people look at you. They are going to see a new level of the glory of God radiating through you. And with your new vision and spiritual sight, you are going to see others differently, too. Led by the Spirit and tempered by the Word of God, you will see motives and intentions of people's hearts. You will be moved by love and compassion and will be restrained by peace and wisdom in all of your dealings with people. Fear, pride, bitterness, unforgiveness, and offense will not control how you interact with people. You will be led by the Spirit of truth and love. Declare it even now.

You have stepped over into a new place in which there is a new outpouring, a new anointing, and a new glory that's coming over you right now, right where you are. It doesn't matter that things don't look in the natural as though they are changing. It doesn't matter that in the natural you're praying, *God, when are things going to change*? I want you to know that in the Spirit, they've already changed. I want you to know that in the Spirit, all things have become new because you are a new creation in Christ. Everyone and everything around you are now going to begin to line up according to the things God has said and spoken into your life.

PRAYER

Father, I thank You for good relationships. Thank You for sending Your Son to model what healthy relationships should look like—even my worst critics. I pray now that You will give me discernment and wisdom for keeping, releasing, or restructuring the current relationships I have. Help me to forgive and let go of hurt and offense of past interactions. I don't want to be led by rejection but by the acceptance and love I receive through my relationship with You. Let all that I do reflect the glory You shine in my life. I declare that I am open to a relationship reset, and I'm willing to release the old. Make all things new, Father. In Jesus' name, Amen.

Reset Your Boundaries

While he was in Jerusalem at the Passover Festival, many people saw the signs he was performing and believed in his name. But Jesus would not entrust himself to them, for he knew all people. He did not need any testimony about mankind, for he knew what was in each person.

—John 2:23–25 NIV

Oftentimes in the Spirit-filled, Pentecostal, and charismatic communities, we talk about boundaries in the context of God's expansion of them. We sing songs about expanding or enlarging our territories, increasing the spiritual space we occupy, extending the reach of our influence and anointing. We want no limits, no boundaries. We want increase and to take the limits off just about everything. We talk about bigger, greater, and mega. We even memorized the prayer of Jabez and made it our daily confession. If you have lived in generations of lack and oppression, or if you have been reduced or dismissed, exposure to revelations like this are necessary to help you see what is possible in God. And if you came from a background where small thinking was the norm, you need to learn to think big and expect bigger. God-ordained, healthy boundaries are not bad things, and limits are important if you are to maximize your effectiveness in the Kingdom.

What Are Boundaries?

According to the American Psychological Association, boundaries are "a psychological demarcation that protects the integrity of an individual or group or that helps the person or group set realistic limits on participation in a relationship or activity."[3] The simplest way we establish our "psychological demarcation" is by saying no. Yet, for many people, especially Christians, no is the hardest word for them to speak, because they think they will be thought of as selfish, unkind, or unloving. The truth is the right no at the right time protects the integrity of who we are and what we have been called to do at a particular point in time.

The inability to say no doesn't really show that we are nice people, it actually reveals our insecurity and, at times, our issues with pride or self-importance. God created us as finite beings, meaning that we are bound by time (24 hours in a day) and physical space (we can't be in two places at once). He created us with a need for basic refueling—we need to eat, drink, and sleep—and with a need to live and work in harmony and community with each other.

You can't do it all. You weren't meant to. When you start to think that you're the only one who can get something done or that if you don't show up it won't happen, then you have to wonder if God wants it to happen at all. We need to respect our built-in needs and limitations, to make room for God to work where we can't, and to work more cooperatively with others in the Body of Christ.

Even Jesus had boundaries, and He was fully God on earth. He had no problem stepping away from the crowds, getting alone, and spending time with God to recharge. Jesus took naps, fed Himself well, exercised, and spent time with friends (see Matthew 26:18, 20, 36–38; Mark 1:16, 4:38; Luke 7:36; John 10:40, 12:2).

There has been a lot of talk recently about self-care. There are important benefits to making sure we are not pouring from an empty cup. Healthy boundaries make sure that we can lead and serve from an overflow, not from a deficit. Let's look now at a few boundaries you need to be setting as God leads you into this new season.

What Kinds of Boundaries Can You Set?

> The boundary lines have fallen for me in pleasant places; surely I have a delightful inheritance.
>
> Psalm 16:6 NIV

Godly boundaries make giving, serving, and loving others pleasant and delightful. When is the last time you heard a leader or ministry worker say that his or her ministry assignment is pleasant and delightful? If you are not enjoying serving God and His people, you may need to reset your boundaries. Something changed for you a while back, and you need to seek God for a recalibration.

One of the main ways to discern how or where to set boundaries is to remember that you are designed to please and serve

God and not people. That may sound a little different from what you have heard. Serving and loving people are good things, but we are to serve and love people in relationship to how God leads us to do it.

What happens when what people want us to do contradicts with what God told us? The Bible says that we should fear God rather than man. When we serve people beyond the limits God has uniquely set for us, we risk becoming easy targets for bitterness and resentment. Boundaries are as unique as fingerprints. What's too much for you may be just right for someone else. Here are a few types of boundaries you can consider setting as God redefines the territory to which He has called you.

Boundaries that limit people's access to you and your time

Our key verse for the day is our main example for this kind of boundary. Jesus' ministry had been exploding. With the miracles He performed, He was becoming well known. I've prophesied throughout this forty-day journey that God is about to elevate you and bring you into a new place in which you will be known for the giftings and call that He has placed on your life. And like Jesus, you will not be able to entrust yourself to just anyone. The Bible says that He knew all people. In other words, He knew what was in their hearts. He knew who was truly for Him and who just wanted to be around Him for clout. God is taking you to a place where you will need to discern who is for you and who is there just to be associated with the things you do or have. People who are not for you will waste your time and resources. Boundaries help you to be a good steward over both.

Boundaries that let you rest and reset

But now even more the report about him went abroad, and great crowds gathered to hear him and to be healed of their infirmities. But he would withdraw to desolate places and pray.

Luke 5:15–16 ESV

You must learn when it's time to pull away from the crowd and rest. Taking time off in ministry can be difficult. People have a tendency to think you should always be available for them. You, however, are not God—and even He rested. Rest is something God instituted at creation, and we see it show up many times in Jesus' ministry. Jesus took breaks and naps. He went away by Himself. He even called His disciples to come away with Him and rest. Rest restores you and gives you a chance to come back stronger. When is the last time you took some time away?

Boundaries that limit the effort, strength, or energy you put into something

Be strong and of good courage.

Joshua 1:9

We've talked about Joshua and the meaning behind this verse on a previous day, but I want to share something new that God recently showed me about the word *strong*. The word carries several meanings we are familiar with, but the one definition that we rarely apply to it is "restraint."[4] True strength knows when to restrain. There are times when you must put all your energy into something, and then there are times when you need to know when to hold back and restrain, when to pull yourself back, when to close your mouth, when to open it, when to say that word, or when to keep that word in your heart.

Boundaries enable us to demonstrate real strength under fire. There are times when you'll need to pick and choose your battles. You can't get into every spiritual battle. You can't allow yourself to be pulled into every situation. You must exercise boundaries or restraint. You must know if you should use your strength or energy on one assignment over another. If it's not what the Lord is calling you to do, then you'll need to restrain yourself, pull back, and say no.

There are times when we allow ourselves to get mixed up in the situations and circumstances of others. The seemingly pressing needs of other people can be a distraction sent from the enemy that will cause you to drain or lose your strength. But you must make room for God to be God in people's lives. While it may not be your assignment, He has other ways of ministering to people's needs. It doesn't always have to be you.

Even as God expands your territory, there are still boundaries He'll set around it to define what He has given you and what He hasn't. He has called you to a certain time, place, and people. You must know the boundary lines of your call. Ask the Lord, *Within what space and time should I operate? Who are the people to whom You've called me? What do You want me to give them? How much of it should I give?*

God's ways to make you an effective vessel for His use are precise. Obey Him, follow His leading, and discern and yield to the times of the Lord. You will find your times of serving Him a pleasure and a delight. You will not burn out. You will not overextend yourself. When you know your boundaries and lines for your giftings and call, you will experience more joy in serving others. You'll become what the Bible calls a cheerful giver (see 2 Corinthians 9:7).

PRAYER

Father, thank You for enlarging the place around my tent, and thank You for making sure my boundary lines fall in pleasant places. I pray that You will help me lean on You and follow Your Spirit to discern who I should serve and when I should serve them. Teach me to pour from a full cup. I come against any spirits of shame, people-pleasing, and insecurity. I do not want those to have a voice in whether I say no or yes or if You've called me to rest. I will not give place to the fear of man. I fear God and God alone. In Jesus' name, Amen.

Align with God's Agenda

See, I have this day set you over the nations and over the kingdoms, to root out and to pull down, to destroy and to throw
down, to build and to plant.

—Jeremiah 1:10

As a body of believers, it is important that we discern the
season. Ecclesiastes talks about the danger of being un-
aware of the time we're in. It says, "Like fish taken in a cruel
net, like birds caught in a snare, so the sons of men are snared
in an evil time, when it falls suddenly [or unexpectedly] upon
them" (Ecclesiastes 9:12). In other words, we can get caught or
stuck in a dangerous place or situation we don't want to be in.

If we are stuck in a place or position in time, we'll miss what
God is saying and doing right now and the opportunities He has
for us. And what God has shown me is that we are in a season
of change and transition, and it doesn't feel good. Things are
being torn down so that God can build up other things. He's
allowing certain structures to be torn down. He's tearing down
the ways we've always done things. Our ideologies and thinking

are being completely torn down so that God can rebuild them for this new era.

Things that were hidden are coming to the surface. Corruption and wickedness in high places is being exposed. While He's starting the exposé in the house of God, it's going to continue in the world. As God exposes the things that are not like Him, you must know that you are safe when you are in alignment with God.

God said to Jeremiah, "See, I have this day set you over the nations and over the kingdoms, to root out and to pull down, to destroy and to throw down, to build and to plant" (Jeremiah 1:10). In so many words, He's saying, "There are some things I want you to do, and it is not going to look pretty." But because of the tearing down of things that God is not pleased with, this will also be a time when we will see the glory of the Lord cover the earth. With pruning comes a greater harvest.

God is cleansing the house. Whenever the Lord begins to prune and clean something, know that He's pruning for harvest. You cannot have a harvest without the pruning of the Lord. Pruning is about judgment, correction, righting wrongs, and balancing the scales. God's pruning brings justice.

You may be coming out of a season in which you felt as though things were off balance, like your world was spinning off its axis. I want you to know that as you press into God during this forty-day reset, you will see things line up again. God says, *I'm now balancing scales.* When the Lord begins to judge, He is righting and correcting wrongs and balancing scales. What was upside down is now being turned right side up. God is bringing things back into balance and back into their proper order.

As things are realigning in your life, God is calling you to stand with Him in your renewed power and authority and to call the things around you back into order. It is time for you to rise up and get back on the wall. You may be looking at things happening around you and wondering what you can do. In fact, for the last few seasons, you may have felt as though you've been in a cave, like David at Adullam (see 1 Samuel 22:1–5). You may have felt powerless and ineffective, as if your gifts were dormant and there was nothing you could really do. Or maybe you've been stuck and just waiting for your time.

Well, I've come to tell you the Lord is activating you right now. He is calling you out of hiding. He is breaking you out of the enemy's time trap. He is resetting your clock and calling you to action, because there are things to which you have been called that no president, government, or system of the world can solve. God has called and anointed you for this season and for this time. When you get in line with God's heart on the matter and get back on the wall—your position of prayer and authority—you will begin to see things come to order.

If there was ever a time to put into practice all the things we have heard, now is that time. We have sat in church for years. We've been preached to and prophesied over. How many more prophecies do we need?

We don't need another prophecy to tell us what material thing we are going to get. We have gotten so fat, and we've not known what to do with what God has deposited in us. You don't need another sermon. You don't need somebody else to give you another five points. You don't need somebody to give you another ten points. You have all the tapes, and you've watched them. You have all the CDs, and you've listened to them. You've read all the books. Now is the time to begin to implement what you have taken in for all these years. It's no longer just a season of eloquent words and pretty messages and preaching until we feel good. Now is the time for battle. Now is the time to come out of your cave.

What cave have you been hiding in? Have you been hiding behind your ministry? Have you been hiding within the four walls of the church? Have you been hiding behind a title? While we have been chasing after ministry positions, trying to get behind a pulpit, or fighting over positions in the church, the earth has been off course. God is calling for His people to get back in position.

Our assignment is not to just have good church. Our assignment is not to come and just get a title. If the Lord has called you to an office, if He's placed you in a fivefold ministry position, your assignment is not to get puffed up and stuck in your office or library because you are a prophet, apostle, senior pastor, or presiding bishop.

If these titles are causing you to be prideful and arrogant or to fight for your own recognition and honor, you need to drop the title and go by your first name. We cannot truly align with God if our ego is competing for a place that only belongs to Him. Christ is the head of the Church, and the Holy Spirit is the giver of gifts. If you are truly anointed and submitted to God, it won't matter what title you have. If you have been anointed, whether you are recognized for the title or not, you are who you are and there's no stopping the flow of your gift and anointing. A prophet is going to prophesy. An evangelist is going to evangelize. An apostle is going to build and plant. It's what we do when we are submitted to God.

You may have gotten stuck somewhere in your church waiting for a title or permission to walk in who God's called you to be. You may have been trapped in a cave of fear or insecurity or in the enemy's trap of not properly discerning the time. But you have launched out on this reset journey to get the strength you need to courageously come out of hiding, to boldly embrace the call of God on your life, and to realign with God's plan. The way has been cleared and illuminated for you, and God has given you a strategy to expand and move forward. It's time to operate. It is time to function.

PRAYER

Father, I thank You for this word that confirms to me that I have not been forgotten. Even though I have felt like I've been on the sidelines, I hear Your voice calling me to join You at the frontlines. I receive Your instruction to get back on the wall and call the areas You've assigned to me back to order. Whether I am recognized by title or not, I humbly accept my unique role in helping You advance Your Kingdom plans on earth. Continue to walk with me, teach me, and guide me. In Jesus' name, Amen.

NOTES

Week 1: Refresh

1. "Metanoeo," *BlueLetterBible.org*, 2023, https://www.blueletterbible.org/lexicon/g3340/kjv/tr/0-1/.

2. See Exodus 34:22; Leviticus 23:15–22; Deuteronomy 16:16; 2 Chronicles 8:13; Ezekiel 1.

3. "Restore," *Merriam-Webster.com*, 2023, https://www.merriam-webster.com/dictionary/restore.

Week 2: A Holy Convocation

1. T. Austin-Sparks, "The Silver Trumpets of Redemption," *Austin-Sparks.net*, 1978, https://www.austin-sparks.net/english/001196.html#:~:text=The%20trumpets%20were%20made%20of,very%20constitution%20of%20our%20being.

Week 4: Restoration Is Here

1. "Kataritzō," *BlueLetterBible.org*, 2023, https://www.blueletterbible.org/lexicon/g2675/kjv/tr/0-1/.

Week 5: Reset for a Relaunch

1. "Purpose," *Dictionary.Cambridge.org*, 2023, https://dictionary.cambridge.org/us/dictionary/english/purpose.

2. "Yāda," *BlueLetterBible.org*, 2023, https://www.blueletterbible.org/lexicon/h3045/kjv/wlc/0-1/.

3. "Hupomone," *BibleStudyTools.com*, 2023, https://www.biblestudytools.com/lexicons/greek/nas/hupomone.html.

4. "Diabolos," *BlueLetterBible.org*, 2023, https://www.blueletterbible.org/lexicon/g1228/kjv/tr/0-1/.

5. "Kérussó," *BibleHub.com*, 2023, https://biblehub.com/greek/2784.htm.

6. "Nabat, H5027," *LexiConcordance.com*, 2023, http://lexiconcordance.com/hebrew/5027.html.

Week 6: Redeeming the Time

1. The Hebrew word for *die* is *muwth*, and one of its meanings is "to dispatch or to send to another destination." "Muwth," *BibleStudyTools.com*, 2023, https://www.biblestudytools.com/lexicons/hebrew/kjv/muwth.html.

2. "Apollumi," *BibleTools.org*, 2023, https://www.bibletools.org/index.cfm/fuseaction/Lexicon.show/ID/G622/apollumi.htm#:~:text=Strong%27s%20%23622%3A%20apollumi%20(pronounced,%2C%20lose%2C%20mar%2C%20perish.

3. "6582. Pashach," *BibleHub.com*, 2023, https://biblehub.com/hebrew/6582.htm.

4. "8609. Taphar," *BibleHub.com*, 2023, https://biblehub.com/hebrew/8609.htm.

5. "6884. Tsaraph," *BibleHub.com*, 2023, https://biblehub.com/hebrew/6884.htm.

6. "3176. Yachal," *BibleHub.com*, 2023, https://biblehub.com/hebrew/3176.htm.

7. "Metanoeo," *BibleStudyTools.com*, 2023, https://www.biblestudytools.com/lexicons/greek/kjv/metanoeo.html.

8. "1247. Diakoneó," *BibleHub.com*, 2023, https://biblehub.com/greek/1247.htm.

9. "Quantum Leap," *Merriam-Webster.com*, 2023, https://www.merriam-webster.com/dictionary/quantum%20leap?utm_campaign=sd&utm_medium=serp&utm_source=jsonld.

10. "Leap," *Merriam-Webster.com*, 2023, https://www.merriam-webster.com/dictionary/leap.

Week 7: Strategic Spiritual Warfare

1. "NIOSH Training for Nurses on Shift Work and Long Hours," *CDC.gov*, March 31, 2020, https://www.cdc.gov/niosh/work-hour-training-for

-nurses/longhours/mod3/08.html#:~:text="Sometimes%20it%27s%20almost %20like%20you,%2C%20this%20could%20be%20fatal.

2. "What Is *Shmita*: The Sabbatical Year?" *IFCJ.org*, 2023, https://www.ifcj .org/learn/resource-library/what-is-shmita-the-sabbatical-year.

3. "*Shmita,*" *BlueLetterBible.org*, 2023, https://www.blueletterbible.org /lexicon/h8059/kjv/wlc/0-1/.

4. "Wile," *Dictionary.com*, 2023, https://www.dictionary.com/browse/wil es.

5. "Gird Up Your Loins," *MBU.edu*, Fall/Winter 2007, https://www.mbu .edu/seminary/gird-up-your-loins/.

6. "Hypodeō," *BlueLetterBible.org*, 2023, https://www.blueletterbible.org /lexicon/g5265/kjv/tr/0-1/.

7. "Endyō," *BlueLetterBible.org*, 2023, https://www.blueletterbible.org /lexicon/g1746/kjv/tr/0-1/.

8. "Hāzaq," *BlueLetterBible.org*, 2023, https://www.blueletterbible.org /lexicon/h2388/kjv/wlc/0-1/.

Week 8: Revolutionize Your Life

1. "Nepeš," *BlueLetterBible.org*, 2023, https://www.blueletterbible.org /lexicon/h5315/kjv/wlc/0-1/.

2. Ibid.

3. "Boundary," *Dictionary.APA.org*, 2023, https://dictionary.apa.org/boun dary.

4. "Hāzaq," *BlueLetterBible.org*, 2023, https://www.blueletterbible.org /lexicon/h2388/kjv/wlc/0-1/.

Joshua Giles is an apostle, prophet, and sought-after conference speaker. He has traveled to more than 35 nations in Africa, Europe, and the Middle East. He is the lead pastor and founder of Kingdom Embassy Worship Center in Minneapolis, Minnesota, and founder of Joshua Giles Ministries and the Mantle Network. Joshua reaches out internationally through apostolic centers, prophetic schools, and training modules, and he has been consulted by government officials, dignitaries, and national leaders seeking prophetic counsel.

Further, Joshua is a media influencer and popular podcaster, with over a quarter of a million downloads and subscribers. His social media show, Global Prophetic Forecast, averages up to eighty thousand viewers weekly, and his weekly videos on his YouTube channel and other social platforms do the same. He has been featured on national TV and media outlets, including the Christian Broadcasting Network (CBN), It's Supernatural! Network (ISN), and Charisma magazine.

Joshua has a double bachelor's degree in business management and psychology, and a master's degree in theological studies. He has devoted his time to helping Christian entrepreneurs, training leaders, and empowering believers. He has a great desire to help others succeed in what God has called them to do. More than anything, it is his ultimate desire to do the will of God for his life. To learn more about Joshua and his ministry, visit:

JoshuaGiles.com.

ProphetJoshuaGiles

JoshuaGilesGlobal